D1111473

"At last, Louie Giglio has put into print the message God birthed in him years ago…a message that has shaped a generation of students, a message that has sent shock waves through the church, a message that has the potential to profoundly impact your worship."

ANDY STANLEY, SENIOR PASTOR, NORTH POINT MINISTRIES AND AUTHOR OF *NEXT GENERATION LEADER*

"I'm not a worship guy…er, so I thought, but Louie's book nailed me. After reading his book I finally 'get' worship. Louie helped me realize that worship is an all-the-time thing, a *life* thing. I was encouraged by this book. Mostly I was moved by Louie's obvious passion for God and his gift for making worship make sense."

MICHAEL YACONELLI, OWNER, YOUTH SPECIALTIES

"Some of the most inspiring teaching on worship I've ever heard has come from the mouth of Louie Giglio. Having read *The Air I Breathe* I can now say the same of Louie's gift to communicate through the written word. This book has inspired me as a worshiper, and as a worship leader."

MATT REDMAN, AUTHOR OF *THE UNQUENCHABLE WORSHIPPER* AND *THE HEART OF WORSHIP*

"Don't read *The Air I Breathe* unless you want to reexamine your life to see whom or what you are truly worshiping on a daily basis. Louie spells it out in plain language: Learning the real meaning of worship is the most essential element in the spiritual journey of the Christian. In the end, our worship is more about what we do than what we say."

BILLY RAY HEARN, FOUNDER, SPARROW RECORDS

"Louie Giglio explores what God desires most in our worship with clarity and insight. Upon reading *The Air I Breathe*, you'll be both challenged and liberated to discover that true worship inescapably involves who you are—all the time."

DR. CHARLES F. STANLEY, SENIOR PASTOR,
FIRST BAPTIST CHURCH, ATLANTA, GEORGIA

"Louie Giglio communicates Christian truth in a wonderfully accessible and relevant way. *The Air I Breathe* is packed full of gems that inspire and encourage. He says everything I would want to say about worship—only he says it much, much better. This is a prophetic and timely book."

MIKE PILIVACHI, PASTOR, SOUL SURVIVOR CHURCH,
WATFORD, UNITED KINGDOM

"This book is a challenging reminder that our worship is for God and not for ourselves."

BILL HEARN, PRESIDENT AND CEO,
EMI CHRISTIAN MUSIC GROUP

THE AIR
I BREATHE

WORSHIP AS
A WAY OF LIFE

LOUIE GIGLIO
Founder of the Passion Movement

MULTNOMAH

THE AIR I BREATHE

All Scripture quotations, unless otherwise indicated, are taken from the Holy Bible, New International Version®, NIV®. Copyright © 1973, 1978, 1984 by Biblica Inc.® Used by permission. All rights reserved worldwide. Scripture quotations marked (NASB) are taken from the New American Standard Bible®. © Copyright The Lockman Foundation 1960, 1962, 1963, 1968, 1971, 1972, 1973, 1975, 1977. Used by permission. (www.Lockman.org). Scripture quotations marked (MSG) are taken from The Message. Copyright © by Eugene H. Peterson 1993, 1994, 1995, 1996, 2000, 2001, 2002. Used by permission of NavPress. All rights reserved. Represented by Tyndale House Publishers Inc. Scripture quotations marked (KJV) are taken from the King James Version.

Trade Paperback ISBN 978-0-7352-9071-6
Hardcover ISBN 978-1-60142-999-5
eBook ISBN 978-0-30756-254-8

Copyright © 2003 by Louie Giglio

Excerpt from *I Am Not but I Know I AM,* copyright © 2005, 2012 by Louie Giglio.

Cover design by Kristopher K. Orr

All rights reserved. No part of this book may be reproduced or transmitted in any form or by any means, electronic or mechanical, including photocopying and recording, or by any information storage and retrieval system, without permission in writing from the publisher.

Published in the United States by Multnomah, an imprint of the Crown Publishing Group, a division of Penguin Random House LLC, New York.

MULTNOMAH® and its mountain colophon are registered trademarks of Penguin Random House LLC.

Library of Congress Cataloging-in-Publication Data
Names: Giglio, Louie, author.
Title: The air I breathe : worship as a way of life / Louie Giglio.
Description: Reprint Edition. | Colorado Springs : Multnomah, 2017. | Originally
    published: Sisters, Or. : Multnomah Publishers, c2003.
Identifiers: LCCN 2017040418| ISBN 9780735290716 (pbk.) | ISBN 9780307562548
    (electronic)
Subjects: LCSH: Worship.
Classification: LCC BV10.3 .G54 2017 | DDC 248.3—dc23 LC record available at
    https://lccn.loc.gov/2017040418

Printed in the United States of America
2019 - Trade Paperback Edition

10 9 8 7 6 5 4 3

SPECIAL SALES
Most Multnomah books are available at special quantity discounts when purchased in bulk by corporations, organizations, and special-interest groups. Custom imprinting or excerpting can also be done to fit special needs. For information, please e-mail specialmarketscms@penguinrandomhouse.com or call 1-800-603-7051.

Anyone who knows me knows Shelley is a vital part
of who I am and all I do…including this book.
Together we want our lives to count for His renown.
Shelley, you are an amazing, God-sent partner in life,
love, laughter, and ministry—in worship.

CONTENTS

THE AIR I BREATHE

THAT THING WE DO

You, my friend…are a worshiper!

There, I said it.

Every day, all day long, everywhere you go, you worship. It's what you do. It's who you are.

So if by chance you have only a few seconds to check out this book, that's what it's all about. We all are worshipers, created to bring pleasure and glory to the God who made us.

I don't know whether or not you consider yourself a "worshiping" kind of person, but you cannot help but worship—something.

It's what you were made to do.

Should you for some reason choose not to give God what He desires, you'll still worship something—exchanging the Creator for something He has created.

Think of it this way: Worship is simply about value. The simplest definition I can give is this: Worship is our response to what we value most.

That's why worship is that thing we all do. It's what we're all about on any given day. Because worship is about saying, "This person, this thing, this experience (this whatever) is what matters most to me…it's the thing I put first in my life."

That "thing" might be a relationship. A dream. Friends. Status. Stuff. A name. Some kind of pleasure. Whatever name you put on it, this thing or person is what you've concluded in your heart is worth most to you. And whatever is worth most to you is—you guessed it—what you worship.

Worship tells us what we value most. As a result, worship determines our actions, becoming the driving force for all we do.

And we're not just talking about the religious crowd. Christians. The churchgoer among us. We're talking about everybody on planet earth…a multitude of souls proclaiming with every breath what is worthy of their affection, their attention, their allegiance. Proclaiming with every step what it is they worship.

Some of us attend the church on the corner, professing to worship the Living God above all. Others who rarely step inside the church doors would say worship isn't a part of their lives because they aren't "religious." But everybody has an altar. And every altar has a throne.

So how do you know where and what you worship?

It's easy. You simply follow the trail of your time, your affection, your energy, your money, and your loyalty. At the end of that trail you'll find a throne; and whatever, or whomever, is on that throne is what's of highest value to you. On that throne is what you worship.

Sure, not too many of us walk around saying, "I worship my stuff. I worship my Xbox. I worship my job. I worship this pleasure. I worship her. I worship my body. I worship me!"

But the trail never lies. We may say we value this thing or that thing more than any other, but the volume of our actions speaks louder than our words.

In the end, our worship is more about what we do than what we say.

EVERYWHERE—WORSHIP

Worship is *the* activity of the human soul.

So not only do all people worship, but they worship all the time. Worship isn't just a Sunday thing. It's an all-the-time thing.

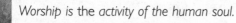
Worship is the activity of the human soul.

Right now, all around you, people of all shapes and sizes, people of every age and purpose are worshiping—continually making decisions based on what they value most. Worship happens everywhere…all day long.

In fact, some of the purest forms of worship are found outside the walls of the church and have no reference to the God of all creation. All you have to do is drop in on a concert at the local arena or go to a sporting event at a nearby stadium to see amazing worship. People are going for it, lifting their hands, shouting like crazy, staking their claim, standing in awe, declaring their allegiance. Interestingly, these venues are filled with the same forms of worship mentioned in the pages of God's Word—the same expressions of worship that God desires and deserves.

A while back, watching an interview Oprah was doing with Michael Jackson in the prime of his career, I was stunned with the reality of this truth. What I witnessed as she showed a video clip of people responding to him in concert settings around the world absolutely floored me. Talk about amazing worship!

In multiple cultures, mobs of people numbering into the

hundreds of thousands were glued as one to his every move. On every continent they gathered like an army, waving their hands in the air. Some fell to their knees. Others strained with outstretched hands, hoping for a brief touch from his. Seared in my mind is the image of one young girl with a look on her face of total awe.

I couldn't believe it. What I was watching was some of the most intense worship I'd ever seen…anywhere. Far more "full-on" than much of what I'd experienced inside the church.

And for what? Granted, Michael Jackson was a legend when it came to entertainment, but he was not a god. Not even close. Yet the worship was phenomenal, demonstrating the God-given capacity for adoration that is rooted in the soul of every man.

And you can see it when your favorite band plays, or your favorite team. People naturally doing the thing it seems we were all created to do.

CONNECTIVITY, PREWIRED

In the same way, we all (you and me) worship something all the time. And you know what? We're really good at it.

If you think about it, history has known no shortage of

worship. The timeline of mankind is littered with trillions of little idols. Every culture, every corner of earth, every age has had its gods. Just circle the globe and watch for worship. Study the great civilizations and explore their temples.

The compelling question for me is, "Why?" Why do we crave something to worship? Why are we so insatiably drawn from idol to idol, desperately in need of something to champion, something to exalt, something to adore?

How do we know for sure that some things are more important than others, more worthy of worship? How do we even know that value, beauty, and worth exist?

I think it's because we were designed that way. We were made *for* God.

The Bible says it this way: All things were made *by* Him; and all things were made *for* Him.

You've been created by God. And if that wasn't enough, you've also been created *for* Him. As a result, there's an internal homing device riveted deep within your soul that perpetually longs for your Maker. An internal, Godward magnet, pulling your being toward Him.

Stamped in God's image, we know that there's something we attach to, something we fit with, someone we belong to, somewhere called home.

*We come from the womb equipped for
connectivity with God, prewired to praise.*

That's why we come from the womb equipped for connectivity with God, prewired to praise. And that's why, from
the youngest age, we begin to worship.

We arrive in this world as objects of divine affection,
miraculous receptors designed to bring Him pleasure. If only
everyone could *know* we've been created by and for God! If
only we could all comprehend that we're precious to Him,
housing mirrored souls designed to reflect His glory.

THE QUESTION THAT
CAPTIVATES US ALL

As I'm writing, my flight home to Atlanta is climbing high above
the Chicago night. Staring out across the horizon, I'm captivated by the thousands of tiny lights dotting the landscape as
far as I can see. Countless twinkling stars of earth, hundreds of
thousands of beacon lights. It's like a sea of little lights—street-
lights, headlights, house lights, neon lights…all kinds of lights.

And I'm thinking, everywhere I see lights, there are people.
People everywhere. A sea of humanity. And every single person down there is someone created with amazing potential

and purpose. All uniquely fashioned to reflect back to their Creator His beauty and wonder. Each one breathing the air of earth in one accord. Each person given life to give Him praise.

And that's only the view in one direction, looking out over just one city, in just one state, in one nation, on one continent.

I'm floored. As we jet through the darkened sky, I think of how this earth is home to billions of worshipers, created to light the darkness with stories of who God is…with echoes of all He has done.

But do they know it? Do *you* know it? Do you know in this moment that you were made by and for God?

While we soar over Chicago, our plane is just a little tiny speck to anyone who might look up and see us, a little dot of light blinking its way through the night. Yet on board this flight are even more people. People everywhere.

Across the aisle from me, a middle-aged woman is digging into a well-worn Bible. (No, I'm not making this up!) She's leaning forward as she reads, as if she knows this Book holds some secret key. I'm thinking how the same God who's worthy of all the earth's worship is the Author of the very pages in her hands. She's holding His autobiography in her hands. There before her eyes is the extension of God's hand. And she's devouring it in large chunks, miraculously forgoing another showing of *My Big Fat Greek Wedding*. It's as if somehow within its pages she has discovered life's very meaning.

It seems we all are eventually captivated by the question of why. Why are we here? Is there a reason for our lives? Is there something we're uniquely destined to do?

It's the age-old dilemma—what's the purpose of life?

The answer begins and ends with God. Simply put, you and I were made by Him and made for Him. You and I exist for one purpose alone—to reflect back to God His matchless glory. You were made for a unique relationship with Him. And your life was designed to be a mirror that reflects all the best things about Him to the world around you. Finding our Maker and connecting with His purposes is the one thing we are all seeking.

Okay, to be fair, things have changed on board. Forty minutes have passed, and the woman across the aisle is now reading a David Baldacci novel, sending occasional glances toward the movie monitor.

Uh-oh. The headphones are going on. I think she's being sucked into the movie.

Apparently, she's seen *My Big Fat Greek Wedding* a dozen times and is having no difficulty jumping right into the flow. It hasn't been thirty seconds and she's already laughing.

(Not as loudly as the guy in front of me, mind you, who with headphones on is loudly giving a blow-by-blow commentary of each scene to the stranger trapped beside him.)

I guess tonight won't see a miracle after all. The "little movie engine that could" wins again. The unstoppable force of *Big Fat Greek Wedding* rambles on. But she still gets major credit for her deep dive into the pages of God's Word. For she—just like the rest of us—is seeking God. And as far as I can tell, finding Him on a plane to Georgia.

(The guy next to me is sound asleep. The lady in front is talking in what sounds like a South African accent. The flight attendant buzzing around is tall and Romanian. A business-man behind me is wide awake and feverishly working.)

And there are people all around you, too. Today as you work out, sit at the lunch table, or study in the library, there are people everywhere.

All these people.

Do they know their lives have an amazing purpose?

Do you?

SOMETHING MORE

I think people know there's something more to life, though I have no clue if they know who *He* is.

A quick glance at history tells me we have always been searching for something.

In the New Testament book of Acts (a historical overview of the expansion of the early Christian church) we find the main character, Paul, entering Athens to proclaim the gospel. Right smack in the middle of the intellectual center of the known world, Paul found Athens to be a "city full of idols."

In fact, he found a multitude of idols to gods of every name and description. But one idol seized his heart, quickly becoming the focus of his message to the Athenian people. The inscription on this altar read, "TO AN UNKNOWN GOD."

*God is always seeking you. He blankets each
new day with the invitation "I am here."*

Even with all their idols and altars, these intellectual and cultural giants wanted to cover their bases, making sure all deities were happy in the event there was something, or someone, more. The altar "UNKNOWN" stood among them, just in case it turned out that another object of worship was superior to all the others.

Intrigued by Paul's teaching, the council of moral overseers known as the Areopagus invited him to speak to their assembly. It didn't take Paul long to get to the point.

"Men of Athens," he began, crafting a simple and straight-to-the-heart response, "I see that you are religious in every respect. For passing through your objects of worship I also found an altar with this inscription, 'TO AN UNKNOWN GOD.' What you worship in ignorance, I proclaim to you."

Paul didn't find a lack of worship in Athens. In fact, there was no apathy in their worship. Just uncertainty. Worshiping people wondering if there was something more.

A lot has changed since Athens of old. Its ancient idols and altars lie in ruins. But people everywhere are still searching...still building altars to everything under the sun. Wondering if there's a God they can know.

God is always seeking you. Every sunset. Every clear blue sky. Every ocean wave. The starry host of night. He blankets each new day with the invitation "I am here."

It's a kind of revelation that is accessible to all—God constantly exposing His creative power to anyone watching. Add to that the internal magnet we've already talked about, and you understand what it means when His Word says God has placed eternity in our hearts.

Somehow, we know He's there. The creation surrounding us tells us there's more to this life than living and dying.

Yet painted skies and a spinning earth aren't enough to tell His story. Heaven's hosts and atom's wonder are a revelation still incomplete. God's face couldn't be clearly known…until His Son appeared—God on the ultimate search, appearing in human flesh. God coming down to restore and redeem fallen man.

To us, ready or not, Jesus came. To us, worthy or not, He appeared. Accepting or not, we find His footprints in Palestinian soil.

It's history. It's fact. It's inescapable. Jesus came. And in His own words, He came to "seek and to save what was lost."

God wants you to know Him.

Searching for Him isn't like looking for a needle in a theological haystack. He isn't hiding. He isn't unknowable. He isn't some mysterious force or philosophical construct that you can't quite grasp or attain.

In fact, the opposite is true. His Son appeared to all in bodily form. Jesus, "the radiance of God's glory and the exact representation of his being," walked this earth in plain sight so that anyone seeking God could find their way to Him.

God's not hiding. He's been looking for you for a long, long time.

Do you know why? Because He wants you to know who He is…and who you are, too. He wants you to know that you're the object of His affection, created in His image, made by and for Him.

He wants you to know that the Unknown God has a name. He wants you to know that the incredible desire for worship rooted deep inside your heart was crafted for Him.

MEET GOD

Standing before the men of Athens, Paul took a deep breath and unfolded the mystery that his listeners had been searching for. He spoke of "the God who made the world and all things in it." Paul identified Him as "Lord of heaven and earth." And this God, Paul said, "gives to all people life and breath and all things."

Men of Athens, meet the God of gods.

Turns out they were right all along. There *was* another God greater than all their idols, higher than all the objects inhabiting their altars.

This God is powerful enough, Paul proclaimed, to invent the whole world and everything it contains. And He "does not dwell in temples made with hands, nor is He served by human hands, as though He needed anything." Turns out, God doesn't live at the church after all. By the very logic of His immensity, He refuses to be contained by any church or structure.

What a shame. I guess we have to say good-bye to the warning we all were threatened with as kids: "*SHHHhhhh! You're in God's house!*" Although I have to admit it did strike the fear of God into me as I considered that the church building was actually *where* He lived.

It does make for a nice image, though. Can you see Him at the door after the service, greeting everyone? "Thanks for coming, appreciate you being here, glad you made it, hope you enjoyed it. Was everything okay? God bless. Oh yeah, *I'm*

God—so, just…bless! Come back to see Me! Have a nice week!"

Is that God? Watching all the cars drive away, turning the church lights off, settling in for a long and quiet week, maybe playing a little on the organ, only to fling wide the doors again in seven days. "Hey! Glad you're back. Good to see you. Come on in!"

I don't think so. God isn't stuck in church-world. He might even care less about us running in the church halls than we think! Why? Because He's huge. Creator. Initiator of all things. Way too vast to be stuck in some building all week. Far too interested in our lives to simply watch us drive away from Him. Much more worthy of our time than just one hour of just one day.

This God is all-sufficient God. He doesn't need a thing! He made the world and everything in it. Paul wanted the men of Athens to know that He's the constant supply of life, breath—everything!

And he wanted them to know that God is near.

NEAR NOW

God is really close to you in this very moment. Right now, He's near. You may not feel it, or sense it, but it's true.

Paul kept describing this huge and limitless God. He said God has "determined" for all human beings "their appointed times [the span of our lives] and the boundaries of their habitation [the details of our existence]…"

And all for what purpose? Check it out:

"…that men [all people] would seek God, if perhaps they might grope for Him and find Him, though He is not far from each one of us; for in him we live and move and exist."

No wonder the whole world is filled with worshipers. Every last one of us has been created with a searching soul, designed that way by God so we would find no rest until we find our rest in Him.

If you've been wrestling with big questions of ultimate truth, don't be alarmed. If you feel at times like you're inching your way through a murky night in search of home; you're not alone. The journey to God isn't like hopscotch on a chalk-lined sidewalk. It's more like a continual reaching for someone our eyes cannot see.

That's why it's comforting to know God is seeking you, too.

He's seeking you so you can know just how amazing He

is. He's seeking you so you can know what you're created to do. He's seeking you so you can find Him and value Him with all your heart.

He's seeking you because He's God...and He knows you can't live without Him.

That, my friend, explains a ton of stuff for us.

For one, it explains why you worship and why you're so good at it. It's why the whole world is worshiping in this moment.

And it explains why Jesus willingly came. He came to connect us to God and awaken us to the possibility of centering our worship on who and what matters most...forever.

3

WHY WORSHIP MATTERS

When the subject is worship, the stakes are high—because worship is what God is all about.

Worship should matter to you simply because it matters to God. And worship matters to God because He knows He's worthy. I know that doesn't sound too persuasive in our me-centered culture, but it's true. Worship doesn't begin with us. Worship begins and ends with God. And God is worthy of all praise, from all people, for all time.

God is the center of everything that exists. Above all the little gods of earth, He alone is the Creator. Sustainer. Originator. Life Giver. Beauty Maker.

That's why every glimpse into God's presence throughout the pages of His Word affirms that God dwells in endless praise.

Notice the angel host of Revelation, never ceasing to say, "Holy, holy, holy is the Lord God, the Almighty, who was, and is, and is to come." Never do they stop. Day and night they proclaim Him as central in all Creation. Without pause they are constantly affirming His infinite worth.

The same is true of the skies surrounding us. As the psalmist writes, "The heavens declare the glory of God; the skies proclaim the work of His hands." Why? Because that's what the starry hosts were created to do—day after day they echo back to God and shout at the top of their lungs to anyone else who's paying attention that He is huge. All-powerful. Glorious. Limitless. They are affirming that the One who imagined their shapes and sizes is beyond our wildest imagination.

And you know what's really wild? This massive God, who has never known any shortage of worship, wants to be worshiped... *by you*. Right now.

It's not that He needs any more worship to be worthy. No, God can't be more worthy than He already is and always has been. It's not that God needs our worship—but that He wants it. He wants it because He deserves it. And He commands it because to do so is the most loving thing He can possibly do.

God knows who He is. He knows what He's worth. And

He knows the best thing He can give us is Himself. So in calling us to prize Him above all else, God is both gaining the praise that is rightfully His alone and causing us to gain the greatest treasure we will ever know. God is not an egotist seeking more than He deserves from us. Rather, He is God, choosing, in worship, to reward us with Himself.

DON'T WASTE YOUR WORSHIP

Worship should matter to you because you are and always will be a worshiper. It's what you do. You can't help it. You can't stop it. You can't live without it. But you can choose where you invest it. You can choose to make your worship count for today and for eternity.

We're created to worship. That's why you and I are going to spend our lives declaring the worth of something. As a result, we've got to make sure the thing we declare to be of greatest value is really worthy in the long run.

For me, I've got to keep making sure that what matters most, matters most to me.

The same is true for you. It's imperative that you find an object worthy of your affection. It's essential that you find a God worthy of your life's devotion.

You only have one life. And you only have one life of worship. You have one brief opportunity in time to declare your allegiance, to unleash your affection, to exalt something or someone above all else.

Don't waste your worship on some little god, squandering your birthright on idols made only with human imagination. Guard your worship…and carefully evaluate all potential takers.

But valuing God supremely doesn't mean that we can't appreciate things of beauty and style, as well. It's certainly not wrong to deeply love another. Nor is it a sin to really be into your profession or to get amped over a trip to your favorite destination.

Enjoying the things that God has made is not a sin, but when we elevate any of these to the highest place in our hearts, we've gone too far and cheated both God and ourselves.

> For great is the LORD and greatly to be praised.
> He is to be feared above all gods. For all the gods
> of the peoples are idols, but the LORD made the
> heavens. Splendor and majesty are before Him;
> strength and beauty are in His sanctuary."
>
> PSALM 96:4–6, NASB

THE WAR FOR YOUR WORSHIP

Worship also matters because every day there's a battle for your worship.

The things we champion—the values we serve—are not choices made in a vacuum. There's a war raging for our worship, and it's been that way since before there was time.

Even before the earth was formed, one of God's highest angels bolted from His presence, refusing to join the ranks of the true worshipers, determined to not exalt God above all. The account records that in a flash Satan fell like lightning from heaven. Exalting himself more than God, Satan was banned from His presence forever.

Yet, having been in God's presence, Satan knows God is central and worthy of all praise. He's heard the anthem. He's seen the glory. He knows the score.

But because of pride, he couldn't bow. And now, spurred on by self, he leads a band of fallen brothers, spreading his mutiny to as many as he can.

That's where we come in.

How does Satan advance his rebellion against God today?

By contesting His supremacy throughout the earth, leading a traitor-race to exchange "the truth of God for a lie" and to worship and serve "the creature rather than the Creator, who is blessed forever." Satan can't stop worship from happening, but he'll deceive anyone who lets him, leading them to empty wells and puny gods.

Let's check back in with Paul. Remember his message to the men of Athens? Remember his audience? The council Paul addressed that day was called the Areopagus, named after Ares, the Greek god of war. Isn't it interesting that this is the setting God chose for Paul to give this address on the real meaning of life? On this day God's words of truth landed in the very arena where opinions battled. Where war was waged daily to shape the philosophical foundation of man's existence.

In the same way, the very fallen angel who challenged God will challenge what God is saying to you. That challenge is called temptation. Deception. Falsehood. Lies. Thievery.

Every moment temptation is there, lurking in the wings (if not front and center) with glittering toys, seemingly soul-filling treats, and what C. S. Lewis called "Turkish Delight." And he's not just trying to trip you; the enemy is striking at the heart of what God longs for from you and me.

Do you know what God desires most from you? It's the one thing no other person on earth can give Him—your affection. Although a thousand other people can do the work, give the bucks, fill the gap…no one else can give God the unique affection that only you and He can share. But just as much as God longs for your love, there's an enemy who seeks just as hard to steal it.

At this point you may be saying, "I didn't start this war of worship—and I don't care to be in it. I just want to live my life, make my own choices, and do my own thing."

That, however, is not an option. Our lives are on loan from God, a sacred trust of opportunities and decisions. And because we bear the very likeness of the Worthy One, every one of our choices is made on a battlefield with heavenly ramifications.

THE LAST TEMPTATION

Jesus faced the same fate. He, too, found Himself in a fierce fight of worship.

Before going public with His ministry, Jesus was led by God's Spirit into a wilderness challenge. At thirty years old, Jesus was preparing for all that was ahead by fasting for forty days and nights. He was learning how to depend on His Father, clinging to Him for life itself.

As His fast was coming to a close, Jesus was physically drained but spiritually sharp. The enemy, no doubt seeing that Jesus looked weary, closed in with three potent temptations.

You remember the first: "If You're so hungry, turn these rocks into bread."

And the second: "If You're the Son of God, leap from the height of the temple. Surely Your Father will catch You long before You hit the ground."

But notice the last temptation. With this one Satan tried to highjack Christ's worship.

The offer: Satan would relinquish all the world's kingdoms if Jesus would bow down and worship him. What on earth was Satan thinking? To ask the Son of God to stoop to worship a foolish exile of heaven—someone doomed to die, someone banished to an eternal future void of the beauty of angels' sounds. Talk about being deceived!

Jesus' reply was clear. "For it is written, 'You shall worship the Lord your God, and serve Him only.'" Leaning solely on the Word of God, Jesus passed the test and quashed the challenge.

Your worship matters to God, as well. If it didn't, Satan

Whatever you worship, you imitate.
Whatever you imitate, you become.

wouldn't care about trying to steal it from God…and from you.

BE CAREFUL WHAT YOU CHOOSE

There's one more reason worship should really matter to you—whatever you worship, you become.

You can worship whatever you want, but there'll always be a last twist to the story: Whatever you worship, you become obsessed with. Whatever you become obsessed with, you imitate. And whatever you imitate, you become.

In other words, whatever you value most will ultimately determine who you are.

If you worship money, you'll become greedy at the core of your heart. If you worship some sinful habit, that same sin will grip your soul and poison your character to death. If you worship stuff, your life will become material, void of eternal significance. If you give all your praise to the god of you, you'll become deluded with self, a disappointing little god both to yourself and to those who trust in you.

Listen to the psalm writer: "Not to us, O LORD, not to

us but to your name be the glory, because of your love and faithfulness." Then comes this observation: "Our God is in heaven; he does whatever pleases him."

Then, by contrast, he describes the idols men make and choose:

> But their idols are silver and gold, made by the hands of men. They have mouths, but cannot speak, eyes, but they cannot see; they have ears, but cannot hear, noses, but they cannot smell; they have hands, but cannot feel, feet, but they cannot walk; nor can they utter a sound with their throats.

Not too high of a score for the man-made gods. But here's the clincher:

> Those who make them will be like them, and so will all who trust in them.

Simply put: We become what we worship. If you don't like who you're becoming, take a quick inventory of the things on the throne of your heart. If you want to become more and more like Jesus, keep your worship focused squarely on Him.

WHAT GOD WANTS
MOST FOR YOU

God loves you very much. But God also loves Himself, because to do anything less would mean not being God. More than any of us, God knows how valuable He is. He knows He's God. He knows He's central. As a result, He values Himself above all things.

No, He's not egotistical, thinking more highly of Himself than He should. He's the only God, so it's imperative that He think of Himself as He truly is.

But God's centrality hasn't stopped Him from loving you with the greatest love known to man. And through the death of His Son, God has made a way for you to return to His loving arms, washed clean and forgiven because of the price He paid at the cross of Jesus Christ.

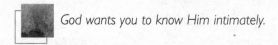
God wants you to know Him intimately.

Where your spirit was once dormant because of sin (sin didn't make us bad, sin made us dead!), God seeks to stir your soul to life again, giving you the capacity to walk in intimacy with Him. Restoring your ability to worship Him with all your heart.

God tells us we were redeemed "that you may declare the praises of him who called you out of darkness into his wonderful light." God loves turning rebels into worshipers— for what could possibly bring Him more glory than that?

God wants you to know Him intimately and to live a life that's fully alive, awakened to His great love.

WHO, NOT WHERE

God doesn't require ornate or elaborate expressions of worship. When we talk to Him, we don't have to use super-sized church words. The worship He's looking for is spiritual and true. Genuine. Authentic. Worship from the heart.

That's how Jesus put it in a conversation He was having with a woman one afternoon while resting beside a common well.

Soon into their talk, Jesus was mysteriously disclosing

His knowledge of her private affairs. (After she mentioned that she was unmarried, He pointed out that she'd actually had five husbands, and the man she was now living with wasn't one of them!) That immediately tipped her off that this guy had some kind of special wisdom. She might as well tap into it, she thought.

She quickly posed a question that evidently had been bothering her for some time. Her people (the Samaritans) worshiped on one mountain, His people (the Jews) on another. Who was right? Which mountain was better? Where should she worship?

For a total stranger who knew everything about her past, this simple "where should I worship" question shouldn't be too hard. Right?

But as we've come to expect, Jesus took the subject to another level, answering her simple "where" question with a riveting "who" answer.

Jesus replied:

> "Believe me, woman, a time is coming when you will worship the Father neither on this mountain nor in Jerusalem. You Samaritans worship what you do not know [think UNKNOWN GOD];

we worship what we do know, for salvation is
from the Jews. Yet a time is coming and has now
come when the true worshipers will worship the
Father in spirit and truth, for they are the kind of
worshipers the Father seeks. God is spirit, and his
worshipers must worship in spirit and in truth."

JOHN 4:21–24

Wow!

After that, I'm surprised the woman could gather herself
to speak, but she did: "I know that Messiah (called Christ) is
coming. When he comes, he will explain everything to us."

(To which I would say, "Lady, you're getting very warm!")
But to which Jesus replied, "I who speak to you am he." In
other words, Jesus was saying, "I am the Messiah, the sent
One from God, sitting right in front of you!" Just the same,
He's right in front of you and me, too.

Jesus has come. Messiah is here. And He's announcing that
worship isn't about where you do it, but about the heart. It's
not about what church you belong to, but whether or not you
have a personal relationship with God through Jesus Christ.

The kind of worshipers God is looking for are those
who will worship Him as their Father—in spirit and truth.

To worship God *in spirit* requires that we be alive on the inside, experiencing the life He gives by spiritual birth. Without His life, you can never truly worship.

And to worship *in truth* means to worship God as He really is, bringing more than our words, but bringing words amplified by an authentic life that flows from being spiritually remade within.

AWAKEN TO GOD'S INVITATION

But how do you get this inside aliveness? How can we possibly worship in spirit and truth when we are doomed to death because of our rebellious hearts?

Notice how Jesus begins His answer—how He begins God's invitation to a whole new way of worship. Jesus opens with the words, "Believe Me."

For all of us, that's where true worship begins. Faith, belief in who Jesus is and what the Father has done for us through Him, opens the way for us to know and glorify Him.

This past Sunday at church I was blown away again by the kindness of God. On this particular Sunday, it wasn't my pastor's message that got to me, though his message was amazing. It wasn't the music. It wasn't even the day's "global theme," though that fueled again my passion for God's glory in all the earth.

On this particular Sunday, the story for me was a woman singing in a small vocal choir backing up the worship band. We were all standing and worshiping to David Crowder's version of "Make a Joyful Noise," and the place was rocking. As we sang, the camera focused on a woman in the choir named Lori. She was passionately worshiping God with a huge smile that beautifully reflected the joy we were singing about.

As Lori's face filled the big screen, my eyes filled with tears.

I know Lori from 7|22, a Bible study I taught in Atlanta for ten years. Geared toward young singles, 7|22 draws thousands of them every week to worship from all across our city. Being a middle-aged mom, Lori didn't exactly fit the typical profile of young people. But her teenage son kept inviting her, and she finally came.

Lori was divorced. She was wounded. And she was spiritually lost.

But she came.

Can you see it? A mom with a lot of baggage walking into a room packed with young people with her teen son...wall-to-wall people going after Jesus.

Something about the place made her feel at home. The spirit she sensed among us drew her in. Pretty soon her eyes were opened to the love and grace of God, and on one spring Tuesday night Lori personally connected with God. Praying a simple prayer, she placed her faith in Christ for eternal life. In an instant she was alive, starting a new journey with God.

Well, that part of the story is amazing enough...but it gets better. It turns out Lori's ex-husband, the teenager's dad, was searching, too. His journey is like so many—a broken childhood and shattered dreams, with deep and desperate wounds leading him down every dead-end road on the planet. In his words, he was "a hard case." A lost cause.

But the transformation happening in Lori's life was too much to ignore, and soon he was opening his heart to the Savior and joining the ranks at 7|22. He, too, became a follower of Christ.

God began to restore the relationship between them, and about a year after Lori became a Christian, they were remarried. They started coming to church on Sundays and both were baptized, an expression of the new life they had found in Christ.

Another God-story! A marriage salvaged. Lives restored. A family mended. And two hearts fully alive to worship the God who made them.

God is always turning rebels into worshipers.

Flash back to Sunday morning at my church. Now here's Lori, in the choir, leading the church to worship the Living God!

How could we expect less from God? He's always bringing the dead back to life. Giving the lost unending purpose. Turning rebels into worshipers. Awakening praise from the pits. Putting a song of true worship in our hearts. Allowing us to worship Him as God…and Father.

It's like David said: "I waited patiently for the LORD; he turned to me and heard my cry. He lifted me…out of the mud and mire; he set my feet on a rock…. He put a new song in my mouth, a hymn of praise to our God."

Watching Lori sing a new song that morning broke my heart with tears of joy.

That's what the power of the gospel is all about.

THE WONDERFUL CROSS

But such a transformation in anyone's life comes at a very high price. God doesn't let us worship Him for free. Our worship cost Him the life of His only Son. Bringing us from death to life required someone besides us to pay the ultimate penalty for our sin.

That's why at the center of all true worship stands a wonderful cross…the cross on which the Son of God died.

But how can that cross be called wonderful? Isn't it a scene of shame? Isn't its beam a place of suffering?

Absolutely. The Roman cross was a cruel and painful ending. It was a place of execution. Rusted nails. Pierced flesh. Searing heat. Gasping breath.

The cross brought open humiliation. Judgment. The cross was agony. A place where people hung until breathing and heartbeats ceased. The cross was where people suffered. And died.

Make no mistake, Jesus experienced the most horrific death imaginable. There's nothing wonderful about how He died. What's wonderful about His cross is *why* He died.

Something truly amazing was happening that day as God offered a ransom for the whole world—Jesus *becoming* sin and shame, suffering and dying for you and me.

To some, it may have appeared that Jesus was being railroaded through the courts of justice and taken by sheer force to die among common criminals. But that's not how the purposed will of God played out.

No one took Jesus' life. He laid it down, willingly satisfying the wrath of a Holy God. He chose the cross in order to demonstrate that God was both loving and just. He gave His life so we could receive ours back again. Men may have driven the nails through His hands and feet, but He died because God was sacrificing His only Son.

The cross was the Father's determined end for His Son. The cross was God's idea…God's redemption plan. The cross was the way to open the door. The cross was the only way rebels could ever truly worship again.

Yes, it's a bloodstained cross. But it is a wonderful cross. In fact, it's the most beautiful thing I've ever seen.

The cross of Christ is a cross of healing. A place of unconditional love. A place of sweet embrace. From His cross comes salvation's song, declaring to all that redemption is here. From it flows forgiveness free. The cross of Christ is a place of peace.

It's the place where true worship begins.

In fact, even as Jesus was dying, worship was very near.

Check it out in Mark's account. A Roman centurion was standing there, doing his job while Jesus choked out His last breath. As Jesus died, the heavens grew dark and the earth shook and shuddered with awe and consternation. All of creation cringed at the sight.

And in that moment, witnessing the greatest act of mercy history has ever known, a Roman soldier—who with his companions had stripped, beaten, mocked, and crucified the Lord Jesus—was compelled to proclaim, "Surely this man was the Son of God!"

Amazing! This supposed enemy of Christ was the first of many to have his eyes opened to God's redemption story. He was the first among us to see the wonder of it all.

In a heartbeat, right there in the midst of the stench and sorrow, worship began at the foot of the cross.

JOINING THE RANKS OF TRUE WORSHIPERS

My hope is that somewhere in the pages of this book you'll find yourself moving closer and closer to the kind of person Jesus calls a "true worshiper," those who worship the Father from the heart with all they are…all they have.

You may be like the woman Jesus met by the well that day—more concerned with your "place" of worship than the God you meet there.

Or you may be like Lori once was, feeling far away from the love of God.

You might be just waking up to the idea of worship in the first place, only now realizing it's that thing you've been doing your whole life long. Only now sensing you need to redirect its flow.

Or maybe you're a passionate lover of God, but frustrated

by the presence of little idols you've kept around far too long.

For all of us, the time for true worship is now. The door is open. The price has been paid. Jesus is here.

MAKING THE MOVE

So while the whole world is busy glorifying who knows what, God is inviting any and all to join the ranks of the true worshipers—those who are beginning to discover the connection between His infinite worth and their own inner longing to love something supremely.

We began this book by seeing that worship is our response to what we value most. That's the basic, entry-level definition, describing the kind of worship everybody does all the time. That definition is like Webster's as he defines worship as "extreme devotion or intense love or admiration of any kind."

But now we're going deeper. Now we're making the move from worshiping any god that dangles in our view to responding to the invitation of the matchless God of gods. Now we're talking about a brand of worship that's lasting and true. The kind we were made for. Worship that both honors God and satisfies us.

For this we need a bigger definition, one that will take us

deeper as we move together toward a life of true worship.

Here we go—

Worship is...
our response,
both personal and corporate,
to God—
for who He is!
and what He has done!
expressed in and by the things we say
and the way we live.

Granted, it's not altogether catchy and concise. But then again, we're not taking on a tiny subject. The definition may be a mouthful, but I like it. And as we dig down to uncover its meaning, it will give us a lot to think about together.

In a nutshell, it's saying worship is a whole-life response to God's greatness and glory.

IT'S SOMETHING YOU DO

Worship is a verb. Or so says worship author Robert Webber.

I think he's right. Practically speaking, *worship* is always

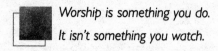

Worship is something you do.
It isn't something you watch.

a verb. Worship is something you do.

Worship isn't something you *watch*, contrary to the thinking of many of us who attend church. That may be hard to believe, given that in most churches the rows of seats (or pews) are arranged so that you have the best view of what's happening onstage. If that's not enough, the action is often magnified on the big screens. The lights also point to the platform. And to help you with your viewing pleasure, you're handed a program at the door—a lineup card for what's happening in today's "show," if you will. After all, it's all put on for your enjoyment, right?

But here's a news flash for you. Worship isn't something you attend, like a movie or a concert. Worship is something you enter into with all your might. Worship is a participation sport in a spectator culture.

Check out the Psalms, both the longest book in the entire Bible and the one that deals almost exclusively with the subject of worship. The Psalms are filled with verbs: Shout to God. Sing a new song. Dance before Him. Clap your hands. Bow down. Lift up your heads. Tell of His might. Stand in awe. Meditate on His truth. Walk in His ways. Still your heart. Cast down your idols. Run to Him. Make a loud noise. Lift your hands. Strike up the band (okay, so that one's a bit modernized). Clash the cymbals. Praise Him with trumpet sound. Seek His face. Tell the nations.

True worship is a whole-life response to God's greatness and glory. A response that taps our mind, our soul, our heart of passion and all our strength.

IT DOESN'T START WITH US

I think the key word in our new definition is *response*.

Worship is our response to God. In other words, we don't initiate worship; God does.

He reveals; we respond.

He discloses; we respond.

He unveils; we respond.

He chooses to show us how amazing He is; we say, "God, You're amazing!"

Our whole relationship with God works the same way:

He loves. We love in return.

He calls. We answer.

He leads. We follow.

IF ONLY YOU WERE THERE

Several years ago Shelley and I were at a youth camp in Texas, hanging out one afternoon by the senior-high pool. (Yes, they had their own pool—middle schoolers once again get the raw end of the deal!) About fifty students stood in the shallow end while four or five of their friends were putting on a diving exhibition at the deep end.

This camp's pool still had a high dive (not too common in our lawsuit-driven culture). And the brave few were taking their turns entertaining the rest. I remember two of them as if I were sitting there now.

One guy was "*so together*." Must have been a gymnast— he was ripped and fit, with perfect "pool hair" and even better form. A typical dive for him would begin with the "Olympic pause" on the very last fraction of the board, then continue with various twists and tucks and turns. Like a missile he would knife into the water, then quickly swim to the side and lean back and shake his wonderful hair as he nonchalantly strutted back to the diving board's ladder.

He was cocky. But he was good.

But another guy was stealing the show. He couldn't dive like "pretty boy" if he had to, but that hardly mattered.

He was robust, full of life, a tad heavy, and sporting yellow surf shorts that hung well below his knees. After each of Mr. Perfect's successive attempts, this guy would appear. Not too bright, but fearless nonetheless, he would fly off the board like mad.

Can you see him? On this particular turn, the guy in the yellow shorts is doing a "watermelon" from fifteen feet up, proceeding to splash everyone in the shallow end of the pool.

Everybody's laughing. Everyone's smiling. He's making the afternoon a lot of fun at the senior-high pool.

But on his next attempt, things turn ugly. Fast.

This time he's flying off into the air with a little extra boost, but it quickly becomes apparent to all that he hasn't exactly thought through this maneuver before leaving the diving board.

Soon he's in midflight, parallel with the water, no more revolutions to take place, and on the way down. Faceup and stretched out, he has lost the battle with gravity—and the pool is getting closer by the second.

At this point I turned my attention to the audience of students in the shallow end of the pool. By the expressions on their faces, I could tell something awful was about to happen. Their eyes were getting wider and wider. An eerie quiet settled over the entire pool.

Then I heard it: *SPLAT!* You've heard it before—the horrible sound of human flesh solidly smacking the water.

At once—as if somehow the minds of everyone watching had been melded into one—a groan emerged from deep inside each person: *UUHHHhhhhhhh!*

It was one of the most together things I've ever seen.

It was as if they were being led, almost like someone had been doing a play-by-play commentary, then orchestrating their response: "Okay, everyone, he's coming down! He's at ten feet and dropping like lead—eight feet, I'm thinking ugly—four, get ready to groan—three, he's gonna hit hard—two, it's going to be a back-buster—one—let's hear it, all together…NOW!"

UUHHHhhhhhhh!

But there was no director there that day telling the students what to do and when to do it. What they did was natural, the most appropriate response to what they were seeing. It was spontaneous. Their response was true.

And no matter how vividly I try to describe what happened on that summer afternoon, I couldn't possibly get you to respond with the same agony and intensity that they did. Sure, you may cringe a little just hearing about it; but to respond as they did in that moment, you had to have seen what they were seeing.

LOUIE GIGLIO

Worship is what spontaneously flows out of us
when we come face-to-face with Him.

LOOK UP

The same thing that was true in the pool that afternoon is true of our worship today. Unless we see God, we cannot worship Him. Worship is what spontaneously flows out of us when we come face-to-face with Him. It's the natural response to all of who He is—our uncalculated response to all He has done.

Sure, we get a massive amount out of the experience of worshiping Him. But at its core, worship is all about God. It's *for* Him. Our worship is *to* Him.

That's why we say—

Worship is…
our response,
both personal and corporate,
to God—
for who He is!
and what He has done!

So often in the Psalms we find expressions very similar to this one: "Great is the LORD and greatly to be praised." When you break it all down, true worship is simply catching sight of the greatness, majesty, glory, and grace of an infinite God.

When God is not greatly praised, it's only because we don't think He's that great of a God. When our worship is small, it's because our concept of God is small. When we offer God little-bitty sacrifices, it's because we've somehow reduced Him in our hearts to a little-bitty God. Our vision has become clouded, our hearts distracted.

As a result, our lives shrivel into insignificance and meaninglessness. We just bump along in this mass of humanity, having no real clue what life's all about. We fret. We get depressed. We worry and get bent out of shape. We go down all kinds of dead-end paths as we try to accomplish everything by ourselves.

We lose sight of the reality of all realities: There's an infinite, limitless God high and exalted on His throne, ruling with all power and authority over the heavens and the earth. A God who's still running the show—running our lives and running the whole universe on His timetable.

And at this very moment, while He holds entire galaxies in place by His power, He also invites us at any time day or night to look up and behold Him as He is. He invites us to call Him by name and be His friend.

FOR WHO HE IS,
FOR WHAT HE DOES

How can we get a better and higher view of God in our lives? How can we become the true worshipers we were designed to be? How can we bring back into focus a sense of how awesome God is?

The answer is, we can't. Not on our own, that is. Unless God Himself shows us who He is, we can't respond to Him with true worship from our hearts.

God reveals...so we can respond...in authentic, natural worship.

So what is He showing us? If authentic worship is the natural response to what God has revealed...then what exactly has He revealed about Himself?

Well, this book, and ten thousand like it, could never contain the sum of His greatness and worth. There's no way we could grasp it all. Our minds are too small. The brain-power is not there.

But there's so much we *can* know. Enough, in fact, to keep us exalting Him for a lifetime.

For now, let's just think about two aspects of His character that reveal His heart to you and me.

INFINITELY AWESOME

We know God is infinitely awesome.

This God with whom we deal is no small fry. He's not our size. Not even somewhat larger. He's not made of the stuff we're made of. He doesn't have to deal with our barriers and limitations.

"Before the mountains were born or you brought forth the earth and the world, from everlasting to everlasting you are God." Notice that the psalmist didn't write, "from everlasting to everlasting You *were* God." But You *are* God.

What does it mean that God is infinite? Simply…that He *is*. Beyond that, our little brains are hard-pressed for more. We don't really even know what "infinite" is all about. Try to define it. Infinite means having no limits. Never running

out. Having no end. Existing forever. Unbound. Timeless. Stuff
we can't fully comprehend.

God has never been tired. Never slept. Never aged.
Never upgraded.

He's self-sufficient. Self-contained. God doesn't need
anything. Or anybody.

If all of us happen to fall off the face of the earth, God
will still be exactly who He is. If all of us abandon our worship of Him, He'll remain the same. God's greatness doesn't
depend on us. If not one single person on earth ever chose
to respond to Him in love, believing in Him and worshiping
Him, God would still be all that He already is, always has
been, and always will be.

> Oh, the depth of the riches of the wisdom and
> knowledge of God! How unsearchable his
> judgments, and his paths beyond tracing out!
> "Who has known the mind of the Lord?
> Or who has been his counselor?"
> "Who has ever given to God,
> that God should repay him?"

> For from him and through him and to him
> are all things. To him be the glory forever! Amen.

Science is gaining ground every day. We can look farther into space and deeper within our bodies than ever before. And what we discover stuns and amazes us. We're finding there's more out in space than we could ever imagine…and more complexity within our bodies than we can understand.

We've put men on the moon, but we can't set foot on Mars, our closest planet neighbor. We inhabit a galaxy comprising billions of stars, of which our mighty sun is average at best. And our Milky Way is only one galaxy among hundreds of billions more, each housing billions of other stars.

We'll never see more than the tiniest fraction of them. Yet God has given each one a name.

> Lift your eyes and look to the heavens:
> Who created all these? He who brings out the
> starry host one by one, and calls them each by
> name. Because of his great power and mighty
> strength, not one of them is missing.

And while we wrestle with the cause of it all, He offers this simple yet irrefutable explanation: "In the beginning God created the heavens and the earth." And why not? If you're as awesome as He is, why not make a universe that's vast enough to constantly echo Your greatness back to You?

But more than just making the universe for His glory, God did it to show Himself to you and me. "For since the creation of the world God's invisible qualities—his eternal power and divine nature—have been clearly seen, being understood from what has been made, so that men are without excuse."

Using the word *awesome*, as an adjective, has become common in the conversations of our day. But nothing is really awesome but God alone.

God is awesome in glory. And awesome in holiness. On more than one occasion we glimpse into heaven and hear the angels repeating, "Holy, holy, holy is the Lord God Almighty." In fact, holiness is the only one of His attributes that we see angels repeating over and over again. Is it possible that holiness is at the heart of God's God-ness? The center of all of who He is?

God is pure. Radiant. Without blemish or stain. He is untainted goodness. Without fault or blame. Perfection personified.

When You're God, You're always who You are—unchanging, unaffected by anything or anyone. He doesn't change with the crowd, go with the flow, or alter to please somebody else.

INTIMATELY APPROACHABLE

And if God's infinite nature isn't mind-boggling enough, consider this: The infinitely awesome God is inviting you to draw near Him.

> "Who is like the LORD our God,
> the One who sits enthroned on high, who stoops
> down to look on the heavens and the earth?"

Yes, He's enthroned on high, but God has lowered Himself to take notice of our lives. To become, as David said, "intimately acquainted" with all our ways.

Think about it. This great and majestic God is totally aware of every single detail of your life. He's God in heaven, yet He knows everything there is to know about you, things you don't even know about yourself.

What a miraculous thing that we're invited to respond to this incredible God. That the Almighty One has somehow chosen of His own free will to desire your worship. Though He had no real need or obligation to do so, He invites you to draw near to Him and discover who He is.

How can it be that God is infinite in being and power, yet you and I can touch Him? We can touch His heart. We can cause joy to come to Him. Cause Him to smile. We can bring God pleasure. Make Him happy.

Your worship matters to God.

It's true that "the heavens declare the glory of God." But right where you are in this moment, God is there and He's saying, "I want you to tell of My glory, too."

The rocks He has made are capable of raucous praise, should He ask for it, but He draws near your side and whispers, "I'd rather hear *you* sing a new song of praise to Me!"

God is constantly surrounded by heavenly throngs and endless praise, yet He says to you and me, "I know your voice, even the thoughts of your heart. And your worship—your arrows of affection—reach My heart and mean something to Me."

TRUE WORSHIP ALWAYS HANGS
IN THE BALANCE

Infinitely Awesome—Intimately Approachable.

Creator—Father.

Lord Almighty—Friend.

A contradiction? No. A paradox? For sure.

That God is Father and Friend at once is part of His divine mystery—something we're better off not trying to figure out. Instead, we need only embrace the mystery, holding on to what my friend refers to so often as "the friendship and the fear."

If we're going to worship God for who He is, we have to continually live in the tension of these two aspects of His character. If we swing too far to the "approachable" end of the spectrum, we'll eventually reduce God to someone our own size, like the T-shirt that proudly proclaims, "Jesus is my homeboy."

By doing so, we'll dishonor Him and forget who we are. Soon we'll be frustrated by this little god we've made for ourselves. Our worship will shrink like socks in a dryer. And our faith will diminish, robbing us of hope and robbing God of His glory.

But we cannot forgo His invitation to intimacy, either. How can we forget that through the wonder of grace we belong to Him as sons and daughters? We are the loved children of God. We get no extra credit in heaven for keeping Him at arm's length. Especially given the fact He has bulldozed His way through the wall of sin and shame that kept us from Him.

We are His, filled with His Spirit. And His Spirit cries out from within our hearts, "Abba, Father." So we consider how awesome He is, standing in awe of all He has done—and at the same time we boldly embrace Him through the life of His Son, loving Him tenderly like a child in his daddy's hug.

AND IF THAT'S NOT REASON ENOUGH

Our worship begins with our response to who God is. But that's not all we have to be thankful for. That's not all we have to celebrate.

Don't get me wrong. If all you ever know about God is what you know right now, you would still know enough to praise Him forever.

But there's more.

In addition to God's infinite character, we praise Him for everything He's done.

Worship is…

> our response,
> both personal and corporate,
> to God—
> for who He is!
> and *what He has done*!

It's the potent combination of these two kinds of praise—praising Him for who He is and what He has done—that cause worship to always be an option for us, no matter what.

When we can't tell what God is up to, and we can't see Him working in our circumstances, we can still praise Him simply for who we know Him to be. Even if our circumstances don't appear to affirm it, God is still everything He says He is. So, no matter what life sends our way, we focus our attention on Him. He's still God in the midst of joy and tragedy.

In that same way, we can always praise Him for what He

has done, though at times we feel we can't quite sense that He is near.

Our lives are filled with gifts from God, little miracles. Flowers *every* spring. The trees that line the road we take to work. The car (new or not so new) that gets us there. A chance to laugh. Eyes to see. A place to sleep. His faithfulness in days gone by. All of these should keep us worshiping moment by moment. Let's face it, gratitude for the gift of breath alone should keep us praising for quite some time!

We praise God for who He is.

We honor Him for all He has done.

Even if God never does another thing for us, should we cease to worship? Of course not—not when we remember all that He's already done through the gift of His Son.

WORSHIP AS A WAY OF LIFE

Which would you prefer?

A dad who tells you how important you are
OR a dad who actually shows up for
the important stuff in your life?

Friends who keep reminding you how "tight" you
are *OR* friends who are there when you need
them most, never stabbing you in the back?

A "significant other" who makes you really cool
homemade cards telling you you're the best thing
that has ever happened to them
OR one who respects you, keeps your trust,
and doesn't cheat on you?

Someone who tells you how special you are
OR someone who shows you?

Well, if you're like me, the answer is…BOTH! I want the words *and* the actions, and I'm guessing the same can be said about you.

Well, God is no different than you and me. The worship God is after is a BOTH kind of worship. He wants our words *and* our actions.

We see this in the two primary words that are used for worship in the New Testament.

Jesus used one of them in His conversation with the Samaritan woman beside the well. This word we translate "worship" is all about an attitude of honor and reverence. It means literally "to bow before" or "to kiss the hand of a king."

The other worship-word has a much less glamorous meaning. It simply means "to serve."

It's the word Paul uses in Romans 12:1–2, a central New Testament passage on worship. He begins by begging us "in view of God's mercy, to offer your bodies as living sacrifices, holy and pleasing to God." This, Paul declares, is our "spiritual worship." Or literally, our spiritual act of "service."

Paul was saying, if you've seen mercy…if you've seen the cross…then offer all of who you are to God in response to all that He has done.

Let's face it: That kind of full-blown serving is not usually the first thing we think of when we think of worship. But in God's economy worship = serving. Worship = life.

WHAT WE CAN DO

What God has revealed to us about Himself is beyond our words of gratitude. What He has done on our behalf makes it impossible for us to ever repay Him.

But what we *can* do in return—and must do—is give Him everything we have through a life of service to Him and to those around us.

That's what we mean when we say worship is a way of life.

For far too long, people have been cheating God, somehow thinking that if they just keep telling Him He's great, He'll be content. Whether their words are genuine doesn't seem to matter. Whether their lives back up their words is no big deal.

After all, words come so easy. And saying (and singing) them makes us feel a little better about ourselves, even when our hearts don't back up the words coming from our lips.

But God isn't honored by words alone. Like any of us, He's moved by words that are authenticated by actions. When it comes to worship, it's the total package that matters—what you say, how you say it, and whether you mean it. And our words mean most when they're amplified by the way we choose to live our lives when we are faced with various opportunities and temptations.

Worship is…

> our response,
> both personal and corporate,
> to God—
> for who He is!
> and what He has done!
> expressed in and by *the things we say*
> *and the way we live.*

On Sunday morning you may be singing with all you've got, maybe even falling on your knees to tell God He's your "all in all." But the whole time God may be thinking, "There seem to be a lot of other things in your life lately that you desire a whole lot more than Me."

LOUIE GIGLIO

God knows how easy it is for us to say one thing and do another.

In that moment, we are no different from those of ages past about whom God said, "These people honor me with their lips, but their hearts are far from me."

God is no dummy. He knows what's going on in our hearts. And God knows how easy it is for us to say one thing and do another. That's why the true test of worship isn't so much what we say, but how we live.

HOW CAN WE OFFER LESS?

God has given us "life and breath and all things," as Paul told those guys in Athens. The only fitting response to all He has done is to give back to Him all that we are. Anything less is not enough. Anything less is not true worship. Anything less only proves that we haven't really seen Him at all.

Take, for instance, His mercy and grace.

We deserved death, but received life. God's grace and mercy are really just that simple.

So how do we respond to the cross of Christ?

With a Sunday visit to church?

By dropping two bucks in the offering plate?

Singing a few verses of a chorus we love?

By lifting our hands?

Wearing a cross?

Owning a Bible?

Showing up for small group a few times a month?

No way! The only right response to such mercy and grace is our *everything*. All our time, all our decisions, and everything we say and are.

I'M THE OFFERING

Somewhere in the modern culture we've become confused, thinking that *worship* and *songs* are one and the same. In other words, we think singing songs = worship and worship = singing songs.

The church scene is flooded with new worship songs. That's not a bad thing in and of itself, but it's deadly when we make a subtle mental shift and start believing that by singing the songs, we're worshiping in truth.

Don't get me wrong. I'm all for worship songs—both old and new.

Singing songs about the cross is fine. It's actually a very

good thing. A biblical thing. Something much needed in the church.

But a song alone is not enough.

The cross demands more.

Grace requires that we bring ourselves, laying our lives before this merciful God.

This wholehearted, full-on, life-encompassing response to God's amazing grace is the "reasonable" thing to do.

Giving God everything is our only reasonable response.

Now, check out Paul's challenging words again, this time from a contemporary paraphrase:

So here's what I want you to do, God helping you:
Take your everyday, ordinary life—your sleeping,
eating, going-to-work, and walking-around life—
and place it before God as an offering.
Embracing what God does for you is
the best thing you can do for him.

That's it! Worshiping God is what we do as we respond to His mercy in our "walking-around life."

It's not the words I sing, but me I bring;
I'm the offering laid at Your feet,
My steps the melody, oh so sweet,
All of me in praise of Thee.

Worship is life!

8

THROUGH JESUS,
ALL THE TIME

As I have continued to try and grasp the fullness of what worship is all about over the years, this passage of Scripture has consistently captured my attention:

> Through Him then, let us continually
> offer up a sacrifice of praise to God,
> that is, the fruit of lips that give thanks
> to His name. And do not neglect doing
> good and sharing, for with such
> sacrifices God is pleased.

We know by the context of the surrounding verses that the "Him" in the first phrase refers to Jesus.

I think the meaning hits us more forcefully when His name is included in the text:

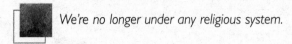 *We're no longer under any religious system.*

> Through Jesus then, let us
> continually offer up a sacrifice of
> praise to God, that is the fruit of lips
> that give thanks to His name. And do
> not neglect doing good and sharing,
> for with such sacrifices God is pleased.

It all happens because of (through) Jesus.

Jesus is the everlasting door by which we come to worship God.

NO MORE RELIGIOUS SYSTEMS

We're no longer under any religious system. Not that of the Old Testament system of law and sacrifice, or any other. In the past, God-worshipers had to approach Him through a very specific religious system of "dos" and "don'ts." But not anymore.

Christ is the final offering for sin; He offered "one sacrifice for sins for all time." So as we come to worship the Father, we aren't required to bring a sacrifice in an attempt to make us right with God. Jesus has already done that for us.

This truth is important to grasp because we consistently fail to live as we should live. And when we fail, the enemy is quick to condemn us, telling us we can't possibly be a worshiper after what we've done.

But those words are lies. We can always come back to God in worship, no matter where we've been or how far we've fallen.

How can that be?

Because we come through Jesus Christ. His death makes it possible for us to be accepted by God. His cross makes our worship acceptable in the Father's sight. Through Jesus Christ we can approach His throne of grace. Anytime. Anywhere.

That's why a huge awareness of the cross is almost always in my mind as I come to worship. And when it's not, the Holy Spirit puts it there. Fast.

NAIL OPEN THE DOOR

How can I embrace this awesome God of wonder and not cherish the cross that allows me to approach Him in the first place?

So many people don't know the fullness of what Christ has done for them…the greatness of who He has made them

*These are the truths that nail open
the doorway into God's presence.*

to be. They don't know enough about their new standing
with God in Christ in order to break free from the
Deceiver's lies.

They try to worship, but condemnation chokes out
their praise. Guilt restrains their hearts. Shame stifles their
songs.

No wonder their worship is weak and frail. No wonder
so many aren't shouting His praise or breaking out in a dance
of unrestrained celebration.

Maybe we're not getting the gospel—the whole gospel.
We're shortsighted and living in far less than we have *in
Christ.*

In Jesus Christ we're free! We are eternally forgiven.
Rescued. Washed clean. Made new. Re-created.

There's no more condemnation for anyone in Christ
Jesus. He's our life. His righteousness is our righteousness.
We're born again. Children of God. Permanently attached to
Him. Our debt is paid in full. Sin's power is broken. Death is
defeated. We're alive!

These are the truths that nail open the doorway into
God's presence. You, too, can come through that door to

LOUIE GIGLIO

worship. Not because of your goodness or righteousness, but because of the cross of Christ.

YOU CAN'T BE SERIOUS

We always come to worship through the doorway of Jesus Christ. But check out what comes next in that Hebrews 13 passage: "Through Jesus, therefore, let us continually offer to God a sacrifice of praise."

Hello! Are you seeing what I'm seeing?

This verse says we are to worship *continually*!

God's got to be kidding, right?

Continually offer Him a sacrifice of praise? Like 24-7? Day and night? All the time? How is that even possible?

Maybe we should all join a monastery. (Or maybe not.) Maybe we should just take a deep breath and consider what the writer of these verses is suggesting.

For one, he's making a massive point with his first-century readers who were quite familiar with the smells and sights of animal sacrifices. They knew what it meant to come once a week, or once a year, bringing some animal as an offering to God.

But it's not like that anymore. We're not talking about a

once-a-week or twice-a-year thing. We're talking about a new relationship that allows us to praise God at any moment, in any setting. In the hallway. In a restaurant. In our bedroom. On a sports field. Anywhere we are.

Continually means that any time is the right time to praise God!

ADJUSTMENT TIME

And *continually* means a huge attitude adjustment is in order. *Continually* means that in every moment, we're constantly looking for ways to glorify Him.

Continually gets our worship outside the walls of the church building.

Continually gets our worship outside of our devotional times.

Continually gets worship outside of our Christian conferences.

Our worship events.

Our music.

Continually gets worship into the marketplace.

Into the boardroom.

Into our hangout places.

Into our conversations with friends.

Into our Starbucks moments.

Continually gets worship into our entertainment choices.

Our bank accounts.

Our hidden thoughts.

Our dark nights.

Our joys.

What God is saying is this: "Everything you are—is Me. Everything you have—is Mine. The life you live is My life that I've freely given you. And I want worshipers who will be constantly reflecting My goodness and grace with that life."

God wants our lives to be a seamless song of worship. God wants our worship to be a way of life.

LIPS AND LIVES

Our continual sacrifice of praise—our all-the-time expression of worship to God—takes two primary shapes. It's made up of words. And deeds.

Let's look again at that Hebrews passage and see where it takes us:

> Through Jesus, therefore, let us continually
> offer to God a sacrifice of praise—the fruit of lips
> that confess his name. And do not forget
> to do good and to share with others,
> for with such sacrifices God is pleased.

The first part of continual praise is "the fruit of lips" that magnify God. That phrase "the fruit of lips" may sound a little odd, but I like it.

There's no fruit without some kind of root. So whatever comes out of our mouths actually comes from the roots that have taken hold deep in our souls. That's why Scripture says that what comes out of the mouth is actually coming from the heart.

Our praise to God doesn't just roll off our lips, but springs from deep down inside us. (Very cool concept!)

God is looking for people who are always soaking in His Word, sinking roots of His character into their minds and hearts. As a result, true expressions to and about Him are constantly coming out of their mouths.

I think that's what David means when he says, "I will bless the LORD at all times; His praise shall continually be in my mouth."

ACTIONS THAT EXPRESS

But verbal praise isn't the only kind of worship God is into. The passage goes on to expand worship to include acts of compassion and integrity, sacrifices that really make God happy.

Now we're moving beyond the fruit of our lips to consider the fruit of our lives.

When we choose to do what is right,
God is worshiped.

And the same principle applies: If we immerse ourselves in God's character, God's character starts to grow "on the limbs of our tree." His character will eventually find expression in the things we do.

For example, when we choose to do what is right in a given situation, God is worshiped. Even if no one else notices or cares, God does. Even if ridicule follows, God is honored. In that moment, God's truth is reflected back to Him. And even if we somehow get penalized for our honesty, God is honored by our sacrifice.

And when we care for someone else, the passage reminds us, then "God is pleased."

It's a lot easier to sing a song than it is to stop and touch the broken. It's a lot less taxing to go to church than to take "church" to your everyday life and to the world. But sharing with others is a sacrifice of worship that makes God smile.

WHAT IT CAN LOOK LIKE

I have a friend living in Afghanistan. He's been there for several years, working among some of the most desperate people on earth. Years of war, famine, and evil regimes have reduced their lives to what they wear on their backs.

Men, women, and children—displaced within their own country. No jobs. No home. No shelter. Little future.

My friend is sharp. Educated. And a believer in Christ. John could live anywhere in America. But he doesn't.

Having abandoned the American dream for greater riches, he can be found most days in some Afghan village...overseeing a relief project, establishing an educational training center, or monitoring a food-distribution program.

He's loving people and meeting their needs. And when they ask why, John smiles a smile rooted deep down in the grace of God, and he tells them about Jesus Christ.

He is more than a missionary. He's a worshiper in spirit and truth. A worshiper in action and deed.

What do you think moves God more? Us singing "Here I Am to Worship" a hundred more times *Or* one undignified worshiper walking the streets of Afghanistan, touching the world's "least" in Jesus' name.

If you've been playing along, you know by now the answer is BOTH.

The song has a place in the worship of the church,

spurring us to lives that are surrendered to Jesus. But at some point we've got to live the song, being willing to go to people everywhere who are waiting to hear about a grace that's free. About a life of purpose.

God loves the world. Every soul in it. He wants all nations to know His name. All people to taste His goodness. Every heart to sing His praise.

But those who have not yet heard of this seeking God will never awaken to worship in truth until we share. Until we worship with our words and our lives. Until we reflect His wonder and grace in every corner of the world.

MAKING THE MUNDANE A MELODY

Sure, you're thinking, *going to Afghanistan is a wonderful thing. But I'm just trying to survive another day working at the bank!*

I understand. Most people are just like you.

No, I don't mean they are tellers. But most people find themselves in places that don't seem all that spiritual. Or worshipful. Jobs that seem pointless apart from paying the bills or filling the time. Circumstances that don't appear to have any eternal significance at all.

If you've ever felt like that, I've got great news. You can

Your attitude of worship can turn any mundane task into an offering to God.

worship God wherever you are…doing whatever it is you do!

That's the beautiful thing about continual praise. Your attitude of worship can turn any mundane task into an offering to God.

Worship can even happen at the photocopy machine.

It did for me.

As a college student in Atlanta, I worked part-time at the Centers for Disease Control. Pretty impressive, huh? There I was stemming the spread of infectious diseases, developing groundbreaking technologies to improve life and alleviate human suffering!

Well…not exactly.

To be precise, I was the photocopy boy in the Centers' medical library. My main activity was making photocopies of the hundreds of articles that various doctors wanted for their personal use.

I didn't exactly have an office—more of a cubbyhole. The photocopier was in a four-by-eight-foot room beneath a stairway at the back of the library. The slanted ceiling dropped below head height on one side. The room overflowed with carts loaded with medical journals waiting to be copied, each having white slips of paper sticking out of them, telling me what to do next.

Hour after hour after hour it was just me and that machine. Day after day the requests piled up. The copying continued.

WORKING, WORSHIPING

But God was doing a lot in my heart in those days, and the job, for me, became something more. I'm not trying to over-spiritualize what happened (we didn't end up having a revival in the library), but by God's grace I was able to turn that copy room into a place I loved.

For one thing, I wanted to be the best copier on earth, never leaving work until every waiting article was repro-duced…something that often required improvements in my technique, speed, and productivity. I would not be denied.

But also, this job gave me lots of time to hang out with God. Photocopying, though manually intensive, doesn't overly deplete the brain. Which left lots of time for thoughts of God. Time to talk to Him. Time to worship. Time to listen. Time to pray.

Everyone working there knew I was a believer, but they

Everything on earth (except sin)
can be done as an act of worship to God.

weren't exactly asking me to lead a Bible study or talk about the Savior. My witness was my work...and work was my worship. The way I did my work was possibly even more significant than anything I could do or say.

I became, to put it modestly, the "master copier." And you know what? I think the way I did my work reflected something good about the character of God.

When I left, it took three new employees to match my pace! And who knows—one of those articles might have contributed to the untangling of some global disease. (For that, you can thank me later!)

The point is this: Everything on earth (except sin) can be done as an act of worship to God. Everything we do *is* worship when we do it for Him, displaying His face as we go. That, by the way, is why we don't want to sin. Because sin is the one thing that cannot be done in such a way that it brings honor and glory to God. In fact, sin is just the opposite. When we choose to do things our own way, we are saying to God, and the world around us, that our God is not good enough to lead our lives and meet our needs. But everything else besides sin can be turned into worship as we do it in such a way as to reflect His character.

Yep, the way you do your work in the office or at school can *and should* be worship.

The way you fry the fries can be, as well, as you manage the drive-through window at Chick-fil-A.

The way you invest your money.

Or the way you respond to your parents or kids.

Or going out of your way to volunteer at the homeless shelter.

These are all a part of what the verse means when it says, "And do not forget to do good and to share with others, for with such sacrifices God is pleased."

The question is not *what* you do, but *who* you do it for.

Your mission is to turn your place in life into a place of true worship. To do whatever you do in a way that will reflect God's heart to those around you.

Your mission is to worship…with everything you say and all you do.

A PERSONAL PATH TO WORSHIP

Developing a personal life of worship is the most important thing you can do. It's where the worship journey begins.

We've talked a lot about our worship being a response to God. If that's so, we've got to keep Him in view, daily pursuing the process of discovering who He is.

For some, I know, that's an intimidating task.

Get to know God? you wonder. *Where would I even start?*

Slowly. Simply.

You take one step at a time.

BIG THINGS, IN SMALL PIECES

The first (and so far only!) real mountain I've climbed is the Matterhorn. No, not the one at Disney! The nearly 15,000-

foot version in the Alps—a sheer triangle of snow-covered rock looming above the pristine little village of Zermatt, Switzerland.

Though at home I'd trained like crazy in the summer heat, I hadn't taken the time to actually learn about the mountain itself. I'd never even seen a picture of the mountain before. My friend and fellow climber, Marc, had assured me it was doable. That's all I needed to know.

When we arrived in Zermatt, what I saw at the valley's end was an intimidating peak of stone. The two angled sides facing the village seemed to rise straight up to a narrow ridgeline top. Certainly no one was going up that way!

At first sight of it, I said to my wife, Shelley, "Don't worry; our way up must be on the back side. There's no way we're climbing that!"

Well, to make a really long and death-defying story short, we did. We climbed right up that imposing face!

This was much more mountain than I bargained for, and I was quickly aware of the fact that I hadn't trained hard enough or well enough to feel any sense of confidence in success. I instantly wished I'd done a little investigating before we arrived. Yet, had I done so, we most likely wouldn't have arrived at all!

In fact, on the main Matterhorn web page, which I didn't check out until we were safely home, is the disclaimer, "Inexperienced climbers should not attempt an ascent of the Matterhorn as their first mountain."

As it turns out, the Matterhorn is one of Europe's toughest climbs, with one of the highest death rates for climbers. It wasn't scaled until 1865—even way back then it was the last of the Alps to surrender to exploration.

That imposing face was swimming in my head as Marc and I tried to sleep high upon the mountain at the Hornli Hut.

Honestly, I had my doubts about the climb.

But we set out for the summit sprint in the early morning darkness—along with our two Swiss guides—and were soon going straight up what seemed like mile-high slabs of unconquerable granite. We climbed for the most part on our hands and feet. And we did it in little chunks—constantly moving, yet only a few feet at a time.

At last, we stood on the eighteen-inch-wide summit of this mountaineering jewel. I wept both tears of relief and tears of amazement. Even more impressive, we made it back down again; an achievement that I now know is far more demanding (and important) than getting to the top. But that's another story.

So—how do you scale something as majestic as Mount God? How do you get to know someone as big as Him?

Answer: a little at a time.

We don't wake up one day to discover that we know God intimately just because we want to. Knowing God—like going up the Matterhorn—requires that we pay a price. And that we take a lot of small steps every day.

But the main thing is to take the first step. In the little book of James we find the promise, "Draw near to God and He will draw near to you." God has already made the first move, inviting you through His Son Jesus Christ to come as close as you want. But you have to respond, telling (and showing) God that you want to be His friend.

To *draw near to God* simply means to take the first step toward Him today. How? A good place to start is with this prayer: *God, I want to know You!* Don't just pray the prayer, really tell God that's what you want most from Him. Ask Him to open your eyes, expand your ability to know and discover who He is, and draw close to you as you run to Him.

At some point you're going to have to carve out some "alone time." With God. Some people call this a quiet time, others a devotion time. But whatever you call it, you are going to need some space that is for you and God alone. Once there, open His Word (after all, it is God's autobiography) and as you read, look for *Him* more than information about Him. Talk to Him as you read His words, thanking Him for who He is and all He has done in your life.

Lay your cares in His hands and ask Him to teach you how to reflect Christ more clearly in your life.

What may be even more important than your time alone with Him is that you walk away from that time fully aware that He is with you, wanting to be a part of everything you do. Don't make the mistake of spending fifteen minutes alone with God only to forget about Him for the other twenty-three hours and forty-five minutes of the day.

In every little step you take throughout the day, keep Him in view. Talk to Him all day long, including Him in everything you do.

When I was in high school I played tennis all the time. I'd practice almost every day after school and then sometimes go home and hit against a wall by myself at night. Those were some of my favorite times with God. Yep. I'd talk and hang out with God the whole time, just me and Him together enjoying life.

But to worship Him best we have to know Him well. A good place to begin is by taking a "Thirty-Day Worship Journey," carving out a few quiet minutes every day for a month to consider one of God's attributes. It could be His faithfulness, patience, wisdom, or constant presence. Or that He's a perfect Father. Or a trustworthy, fair, and encouraging Savior. But whatever aspect of His character you choose, you're going to carry that characteristic of God with you all day long.

Say you start with God's faithfulness, choosing to praise Him because in every situation He remains the same. For the whole day, *Faithful* will be foremost in your thoughts! You're going to chew it up, digest it, meditate on it, talk to God about it, journal some thoughts about it, think about it a little more, ponder it, respond to it, imitate it, be influenced by it, pray about it, appreciate it, and go to bed thanking God for it. You might even dream about it. And you know what? After thirty days you'll be amazed at how much better you know Him. He won't just be this huge, generic "God" to you. He'll be someone you're really getting to know as you begin to discover the fullness of who He is.

It's a little like high school biology. If you've been there you know what I'm talking about—*the frog*! How can you forget? First there's the disgusting smell of the formaldehyde they keep it in. Yikes! Then there's the frog. No one is sure how he (or she) died, just that it's dead and now is being cut open so we can see its insides and identify all its parts. It's both gross and fascinating at the same time, but the point is this: Your knowledge of the frog can consist of knowing that it goes "Ribbet" and can jump a long way *OR* you can really know the frog by understanding its various parts and how it's made.

Okay, maybe that wasn't such a good example, but you get the point. We don't just want to know that God is really "awesome" (just about the only adjective it seems we American's can think of to describe Him) and that He lives in heaven. We want to know everything we can about Him. And here's the best part—we're not just gathering information about God, we actually get to have a personal relationship with Him.

The psalmist said it this way, "Taste and see that the LORD is good; blessed is the man who takes refuge in him." Obviously, David wasn't being literal in his invitation, but the principles of "tasting and seeing" that God is good are what we're going for. To taste begins with both hunger on our part

Begin each day with the prayer, "God, I am here for You, please show me who You are."

and something appealing that's before us. Next you take a bite. It's not advisable (nor possible in most cases) to consume the whole of something in one gulp. Tasting starts with just one bite—a bite you chew well, savor, and then swallow. Tasting leads to savoring, which leads to swallowing, which leads to ingesting, which leads to digesting. Amazingly, at some point that bite becomes a part of you and you become a part of it.

So, here's how it works: First, get a blank journal and begin each day for thirty days (it's been said doing anything for thirty days—good or bad—helps form a habit) with the prayer, "God, I am here for You, please show me who You are." Open to the Psalms and begin to read. The goal here is quality, not quantity. You may be content with a verse or two, or you may want to focus on a whole Psalm. But don't speed along. Let the words sink in.

As you read, look for one attribute of God that seems to grab your attention. An attribute is simply something that's true about God. A part of His character. A facet of His heart. One of His names.

Maybe you'll be drawn to His mercy. Or His consistency. His love. His holiness.

Maybe your heart will zero in on the fact that He's your Sustainer. Shepherd. Shelter. Friend.

When you feel like one thing has captured your heart, write that attribute on the top of your journal page. You might want to write the verse down, too.

Now take some time to meditate on that aspect of God's character. For example, think about what it means that God is wise. That He embodies "all the treasures of wisdom and knowledge." And think about what God's wisdom means to your life today.

After a few minutes, write your thoughts to God. You might write your own psalm of praise back to Him, or just a stream of thoughts as they spill over from your heart to His.

You might write a new song, or just sing one you already know that magnifies the dimension of His heart that you're focusing on.

Make it personal. Intimate. Honest.

Remember, there's no right or wrong way to journal your response to what you see of Him. Two sentences can be as powerful as two pages.

You'll be encouraged at how far along
you are on the path of knowing Him.

Now carry that word with you all day long. Keep the conversation with God going everywhere you go.

You might be surprised how many times that characteristic surfaces as you walk through your day.

Every time it does, thank Him for the truth that He has shown you. Praise Him for who He is.

After thirty days, you'll be encouraged at how far along you are on the path of knowing Him. And you'll be amazed at how much more there is of Him to explore.

GETTING CLOSER IS THE KEY

I don't guess you'd be too surprised to know I have a huge print of the Matterhorn hanging on my office wall. And a large-edition coffee-table book about the mountain is at my house.

More than one unsuspecting visitor to our home has been subjected to my way-too-long tales about the climb, as section by section this book records the very route of our ascent in full-page photos that take your breath away.

When I first picked up the book in a shop in Zermatt, I was totally unnerved by the immensity of the mountain captured in the images. Then, as I looked more closely at what I first thought were shots of the mountain alone, I could see antlike men, climbers within the rocks. Barely visible dots making their way slowly up the mountain. The closer I looked, the more little people I found.

"Over there, three more. And look right here, six more going up."

I discovered this giant rock is a little deceiving. From a distance the Matterhorn looks smooth and sheer. But once you actually get on the mountain you discover it's jagged. Full of cracks and crevices. Little places to get a foothold, or a toehold, as you make your way to its peak.

In the same way, there are endless crevices in the character of God. When we break His Word into little chunks, we find a lot of places to settle. Hidden places, offering good footing as we seek to know Him more.

MOVING BEYOND ME,
TO US

Worship is a personal thing. But it's also something we do together.

In other words, our responses of worship to God are both personal and corporate. And each kind of response is intertwined with the other.

That's why we say:

Worship is…
our response,
both personal and corporate,
to God—
for who He is!
and what He has done!
expressed in and by the things we say
and the way we live.

Christianity is not an individual sport so much as it is a family affair. Through Christ we've been reconnected to God, and in Him we're linked to each other. We are His body. His people. His family. His representatives in the world.

Each one of us plays a unique role. We fit with the body in a necessary way.

I'm not talking about joining organized religion, but the organism called the church. If you're a believer in God, He has made you a part of His body, His people. It's really not your call, but His. He has already made you a member. And a part of your worship is to make a connection with other believers around you.

The primary purpose of the church (the people of God) is worship. At its core, the church exists to glorify God. And without your life and voice, the body's expression is incomplete.

But even in the corporate setting, worship doesn't begin with a group activity. It begins with our individual responses to what God has revealed to us about Himself. Those responses don't just happen once a week...they happen day by day.

We aren't designed to operate on a weekly worship cycle, but on a moment-by-moment connection of personal worship that's as much a part of our lives as the air we breathe.

The primary purpose of His
church is worship.

PUTTING IT ALL TOGETHER

As we come together with other believers in worship, we bring that same sense of focus we've had in our daily journey. We bring that same determined devotion.

Most of my life, I thought that you went to church to worship. But now I see that the better approach is to *go worshiping to church.*

Trust me, church is a lot better when our gatherings are filled with people who have been pursuing God for six days before they get there. Church as a "refill" or a "tank-up" is a disaster. Corporate worship works best when we arrive with something to offer God. As opposed to only coming to get something for ourselves from God. Sure, it is true that we are strengthened and refreshed by what happens when we worship with other believers, but leaning on Sunday as our only time of spiritual intake is a recipe for languid worship and an anemic Body.

Church is supposed to be a celebration of our personal journeys with God since we were last together.

Imagine what would happen if each person in the

congregation was seeking the face of God throughout the week. Some would encounter sorrow, others major happiness. But all would have a story to tell of God's faithfulness in good times and bad.

What would happen if we came worshiping to church, filled with an awareness of His presence before we even reached the door? Well, for one, the lead worshiper's job would be a lot easier! And the intensity of our collective offering would be full-on.

Can you see it? All of our personal streams of worship flowing into one surging river. One mighty anthem. A beautiful mosaic, telling an even greater story of who God is and what He's done.

People leave a gathering like that inspired to seek Him as never before. And they come back again bringing worship with them, starting the cycle all over again.

The worship circle is complete. Unbroken.

CONNECTING THE DOTS

We need to overhaul the way we view the Sunday service. Or whenever it is we meet together with others to worship.

Usually no one has given the service a moment's

thought until they arrive. We come through the door like we're stopping at the mall. We sit and chat. We wait for someone to guide us before we ever stop and connect with the privilege of it all.

Yet the corporate gathering is a sacred thing. A special thing. A holy thing. Maybe we need bigger buildings after all. Cathedrals that remind us that we're really small and God is really big. Buildings that force us to look up.

Dr. Bruce Leafblad, one of the major early shapers of my understanding of worship, has a great definition of worship. Part of it goes like this: "Worship is centering our mind's attention and our heart's affection on the Lord."

You can't make it any clearer than that.

True worship requires our attention. I know that's difficult in our commercial-driven culture, where our television-trained minds have geared us for a break every seven minutes. But God requires us to love Him with all our minds. His sheer scope and beauty demand our complete attention.

Have you ever been talking with somebody who was constantly looking around while they were talking to you, checking out the scene while you tried to make your point? It makes you just want to walk away, doesn't it?

Why do we think it's any different with God?

*It's imperative that we find God
and lock our gaze with His.*

When we come to worship together it's imperative that
we find God and lock our gaze with His. That's not easy with
all the other people in the room. But our primary reason for
being there is to see Him. At least it should be.

I don't know about you, but my attention wanders like
crazy. For me, the corporate worship experience is a constant "roundup," me chasing down my drifting thoughts and
reattaching them to God. So I'm not saying it's easy to stay
focused on Him. Just that it's essential.

FACE-TO-FACE, EYE-TO-EYE

As we worship with others, it's important that we find Him,
because our attention aims our affection.

We have the amazing potential to shoot arrows of
affection into the heart of God. If those arrows are going to
hit the target, we have to know where the target is.

And if those arrows from our hearts are going to regis-
ter with His, they have to be honest and true.

That means we have to think carefully about what we're

saying…what we're singing. And who we're singing to. Sometimes we would be better off saying nothing than standing there lying to the face of God. Our worship would honor Him more if we just stopped singing and realigned our heart with His.

I believe for this to happen we have to connect with God before we arrive. Worship is an intentional thing. It's something we set our hearts to do. So the next time you come to worship with other believers, take a deep breath as you cross the parking lot. Think about the vastness of the God you are coming to meet. Think about His love and grace as you pass through the doors.

And before the worship service begins, begin to worship in your heart.

The key is to come prepared. To come worshiping. To connect with God. To keep your eyes on Him.

WORSHIP IS SO MUCH MORE

You are a worshiper. It's what you do. And you *are* going to worship—no matter what! That's the simple truth of this little book.

Something's going to grab your affection. Someone is going to captivate your heart and mind. One thing is going to rise to the surface of your values and drive your life, aiming your steps and determining your destiny.

It's not an option, no matter who you are. You have heavenly fibers holding you together, a sense of the Divine coursing through your veins. You and I were made for this one thing, and worship is what we will do with our dying breath.

The question we have asked repeatedly in these pages is, "Will your worship be spent on what matters most?" If God is who He says He is, there is no competition. He is unrivaled. He is central. He is most spectacular. Most enduring. Intrinsically valuable beyond compare. And, what's more, He alone satisfies the depths of our souls.

Thankfully, the invitation of God has come to you, opening a way for you to join those who glorify Him with all of who they are. He's inviting you to discover His infinite worth and giving you the privilege of exalting Him as infinitely worthy.

Through Christ, you can breathe again, inhaling the wonder of God that always surrounds you, exhaling words and deeds of praise that reflect all of who He is.

So, whether personal or corporate, let's make this what we do. Let's give Him all we are. When we do, our lives will take on the weight of eternity, being forever linked to His unending glory.

MY THANKS

Obviously, my worship journey has been shaped and shared by countless others.

Just to mention a few…

Thanks to Sam Perry and Shelley Nirider—and many others who joined our team—early explorers of worship with Shelley and me at Choice Bible Study, Baylor University (1985–95)…the place most of these ideas came to life. As well as Chris Tomlin, Charlie Hall, David Crowder, Matt Redman, and a host of other young lead worshipers, friends, and partners who will shepherd the church for years to come.

Thanks to all at Multnomah Publishers, including Thomas Womack, and the staff of Passion Conferences, especially my assistant, Jennifer Hill.

QUESTIONS FOR GROUP DISCUSSION

CHAPTER 1: THAT THING WE DO

1. This first chapter defines worship as "our response to what we value most" and says it "tells us what we value most." Is this a new or larger way of looking at worship for you? In what ways does it make you question or rethink the way you've viewed worship before? Talk openly about this.

2. This chapter also asserts that *all* of us are *always* worshiping. How have you recognized this to be true in your life or the lives of those around you? Can you see it in your choices and actions over the past twenty-four hours?

3. For most people you know, what would you say appear to be the most common objects of their worship, other than God?

4. How can we go about deciding—in an honest and thorough way—what it is we value most in life? How do we effectively and accurately "follow the trail" in order to evaluate how we spend our time? Our affection? Our energy? Our money? Our allegiance?

5. Scriptures to explore: Colossians 1:15–17; John 1:1–3; 1 Corinthians 8:5–6.

Chapter 2: Something More

1. In what memorable ways in your life have you seen that God has been searching for you? How have you noticed His "internal magnet" at work inside you? How have you been aware that He's placed eternity in your heart?

2. Are you fully convinced that God wants you to know who He is and what He's like? Why or why not?

3. In what times of your life have you wrestled most with questions of "ultimate truth"?

4. Talk about the ways in which you identify with the following statement from this chapter: "The journey to God isn't like hopscotch on a chalk-lined sidewalk. It's more like an awkward groping for someone our eyes cannot see."

5. Think about all that Paul told the Athenians. Which parts of his message to them are most meaningful to you, and why?

6. Scriptures to explore: Ecclesiastes 3:11; Hebrews 1:1–3; Acts 17:15–34.

CHAPTER 3: WHY WORSHIP MATTERS

1. *Worship is what God is all about...and God is what*

worship is all about. Discuss what those statements mean to you, and your response to them.

2. Knowing that there's a "war" for our worship—that an enemy seeks to steal the love that God longs to receive uniquely from each one of us—how should that affect our thinking about worship and our approach to worship?

3. In what situations can you most easily recognize the battle going on for your values and for your worship?

4. We're encouraged in this chapter to "guard" our worship so that we don't squander it "on idols made only with human imagination." What are the best ways to guard our worship?

5. Scriptures to explore: Matthew 4:1–11; Psalm 115:1–8; Revelation 4:8.

CHAPTER 4: WHAT GOD WANTS MOST FOR YOU

1. How can God think so highly of Himself and not be egotistical or conceited?

2. "God wants you to know Him intimately," this chapter reminds us, "and to live a life that's fully alive, awakened to His great love." What does this tell you most about God? About you?

3. What helps you most to understand and appreciate how the cross is wonderful? How have you experienced more meaningful worship because of understanding this? How would you describe the place that the cross should have in our worship?

4. As Jesus talked to the Samaritan woman about worship, He began with the words, "Believe Me...." In our lives, how much does true worship depend on our believing God?

5. Think again about all that Jesus told this woman. Which parts of His message to her are most meaningful to you, and why?

6. Scriptures to explore: John 4:5–26; Mark 15:33–39; Hebrews 10:22.

CHAPTER 5: JOINING THE RANKS OF TRUE WORSHIPERS

1. This chapter tells us that God is the one who initiates worship, not us. What practical difference do you think this makes?

2. Scriptures to explore: Psalm 95; 150.

CHAPTER 6: FOR WHO HE IS, FOR WHAT HE DOES

1. What are your best answers for the three questions that this chapter begins with: "How can we recover a more exalted view of God in our lives? How can we become the true worshipers we were designed to be? How can we bring back into focus a sense of how awesome God is?"

2. When have you been most captivated and excited about God's character—about who He is?

3. When have you been most captivated and excited about God's actions—about what He has done or is doing?

4. What have you found to be the most important factors in protecting and nurturing the intimacy of your relationship with God?

5. Scriptures to explore: Psalm 90:1–2; Romans 11:33–36; Psalm 113; Romans 8:15.

Chapter 7: Worship as a Way of Life

1. Think about the word *service*. What kind of thoughts and impressions—either positive or negative—does it bring to mind?

2. What motivates you most to want to offer yourself fully to God?

3. This chapter includes this statement: "Grace requires that we bring ourselves, laying our lives before this merciful God." Is grace really grace if it has this or any requirement attached to it? What do you think?

4. How can we know that we're genuinely honoring God and pleasing Him? How can we be sure?

5. Scriptures to explore: Romans 6:13; 12:1–2.

Chapter 8: Through Jesus, All the Time

1. Why is it so important to keep in our minds and hearts the fact that worship is "through Jesus"? Why does it matter? And what does it mean personally for you to do this?

2. In this book's first chapter, we explored the reality that all of us worship all the time (according to the basic, universal meaning of "worship"). Now as we discover more about the true worship that pleases God, we see Him asking us to worship Him "continually." To offer true worship continually to God, does it help knowing that you're already constantly worshiping anyway?

3. What do you recognize as the most important adjustments needed in your life in order to more continually offer worship to God?

4. Scriptures to explore: Hebrews 13:15; John 14:6; 15:4–5; Colossians 3:17.

Chapter 9: Lips and Lives

1. What specific forms of "doing good" and "sharing with others" has God given you the opportunity and privilege to live out? How have you sensed God's pleasure in this?

2. What does worshiping God mean—or what *could* it mean—in your own place of work or school?

3. What needs in the lives of people around you seem most urgent to you? What needs in the world around you tend to weigh down your own heart the most?

4. What specific "sacrifices" do you believe God is calling you to make in your life at this time, in order to bring blessing to Him and to people around you?

5. Scriptures to explore: Hebrews 13:15–16; 1 Peter 2:5; Philippians 2:12–16.

Chapter 10: A Personal Path to Worship

1. Talk about one or two facets of God's character that have meant the most to you in recent days. How did these come to your attention? How have you grown in your understanding of God?

2. What helps you most to sense that you're drawing close to God?

3. Scriptures to explore: John 1:18; 2 Corinthians 4:6; Psalm 27:8; 67:1–2.

Chapter 11: Moving Beyond Me, to Us

1. This chapter talks about the need to "go worshiping to church." Is this something you experience in your life? What makes it harder (or easier) for you to come worshiping to church?

2. When do you think it might be appropriate in a corporate worship setting to be silent and not join in with others who are singing and praising God together?

3. How can we keep from being more interested in our experiences of worship than we are in experiencing God Himself?

4. This chapter paints a picture of a congregation that truly seeks God during the week before coming together on Sunday. To what degree is this already happening in your church? What can help cause it to happen more and more?

5. Scriptures to explore: Isaiah 26:8; Psalm 33:1–5; 34:3; 148; Revelation 4:11; 5:12.

QUOTATION SOURCES

CHAPTER 1: THAT THING WE DO

All things were made by Him and all things were made for
   Him—John 1:3; Romans 11:36; 1 Corinthians 8:6;
   Colossians 1:16.

CHAPTER 2: SOMETHING MORE

The account of Paul in Athens is found in Acts 17:15–34.

God has placed eternity in our hearts—Ecclesiastes 3:11.

Jesus came to "seek and to save that which was lost"
   —Luke 19:10.

Jesus "the radiance of God's glory…"—Hebrews 1:3.

CHAPTER 3: WHY WORSHIP MATTERS

"Holy, holy, holy is the Lord God…"—Revelation 4:8.

"The heavens declare the glory of God…."—Psalm 19:1.

Satan falling like lightning—Luke 10:18.

Satan exalting himself more than God—Isaiah 14:13–15.

To exchange "the truth of God for a lie"; "the creature rather than the Creator…."—Romans 1:25, NASB.

The account of Jesus being tempted by the enemy in the wilderness is found in Matthew 4:1–11.

"Not to us, O LORD, not to us…."; "But their idols are silver and gold…."; "Those who make them will be like them…."—Psalm 115:1–8.

CHAPTER 4: WHAT GOD WANTS MOST FOR YOU

That we might "declare the praises of him who called you out of darkness…"—1 Peter 2:9.

The account of the conversation beside the well between Jesus and the Samaritan woman is found in John 4:1–26.

David said: "I waited patiently for the LORD…" —Psalm 40:1–3.

"The Wonderful Cross"—this phrase is used in a Chris Tomlin adaptation of the classic worship song "When I Survey the Wondrous Cross" (Isaac Watts, 1707;

adaptation by Chris Tomlin in *The Noise We Make*, sixstepsrecords/Sparrow Records, 2001).

Jesus *becoming* sin and shame—2 Corinthians 5:21.

The centurion saying, "Truly this man was the Son of God!" —Mark 15:39.

CHAPTER 5: JOINING THE RANKS OF TRUE WORSHIPERS

"True worshipers"—John 4:23.

"Great is the LORD and greatly to be praised"—Psalms 18:3; 29:2; 45:1; 48:1; 96:4; 104:1, NASB.

CHAPTER 6: FOR WHO HE IS, FOR WHAT HE DOES

"Before the mountains were born..."—Psalm 90:2.

"Oh, the depth of the riches..."—Romans 11:33–36.

"Lift your eyes and look to the heavens..."—Isaiah 40:26.

"In the beginning God created..."—Genesis 1:1.

"For since the creation of the world God's invisible qualities..."—Romans 1:20.

"Holy, holy, holy is the Lord God Almighty"
—Revelation 4:8; Isaiah 6:3.

"Who is like the LORD our God…"—Psalm 113:5–6.

As David said, "intimately acquainted"—Psalm 139:3, NASB.

"The heavens are telling of the glory of God"
—Psalm 19:1, NASB.

The rocks He has made are capable of raucous praise
—Luke 19:40.

His Spirit cries out from within our hearts, "Abba! Father!"
—Romans 8:15; Galatians 4:6. In Aramaic (the
common language used in Jesus' day), *Abba* is an
endearing term of closeness and intimacy that a child
would use for his dad.

CHAPTER 7: WORSHIP AS A WAY OF LIFE

"These people honor me with their lips…"
—Matthew 15:8.

God has given us "life and breath and all things"
—Acts 17:25, NASB.

The "reasonable" thing to do—Romans 12:1, KJV.

Contemporary paraphrase, Romans 12:1—*The Message*.

"It's not the words I sing, but me I bring"
    —Louie Giglio, 2001.

Chapter 8: Through Jesus, All the Time

"Through Him then, let us continually offer…"
    —Hebrews 13:15, NASB.

Christ offered "one sacrifice for sins for all time"
    —Hebrews 10:12, NASB.

"Through [Jesus] then, let us continually offer…"
    —Hebrews 13:15–16.

Chapter 9: Lips and Lives

"Through Jesus, therefore, let us continually offer…"
    —Hebrews 13:15–16.

What comes out of the mouth is actually coming from the
    heart—Matthew 15:18.

David says, "I will bless the LORD at all times…"
    —Psalm 34:1, NASB.

Chapter 10: A Personal Pathway to Worship

"Draw near to God…"—James 4:8, NASB.

The psalmist said it this way, "Taste and see…"
—Psalm 34:8.

"All the treasures of wisdom and knowledge"
—Colossians 2:3.

Chapter 11: Moving Beyond Me to Us

Bruce Leafblad's definition in full (as given in his course
"Introduction to Church Music" at Southwestern
Baptist Theological Seminary, 1983): "Worship is
communion with God in which believers, by grace,
center their mind's attention and their heart's affection
on the Lord, humbly glorifying God in response to His
greatness and His Word."

I AM NOT BUT I KNOW I AM

by Louie Giglio

[Here. Now.]

Start

Welcome to the book with the quirky title—*I Am Not but I Know I AM*. If you're like most people, you looked at the words on the cover once or twice (or more) before (a) the meaning settled on you, or (b) out of curiosity you picked up the book to figure out what in the world this seemingly contradictory title is all about. Thankfully, you didn't

(c) become so confused that you quietly put the book down (or passed it by on your e-book store) and went on your way.

I'm really glad you made it this far because I believe that soon this crazy title will be making perfect sense to you. And I hope that the truth it represents will soon be flooding your heart with a God-sized dose of rest and meaning, redefining who you are in the very best way. I can only pray that happens in you, because it was one of the best things that ever happened to me.

As for the offbeat title, the thought of it hit me mid-stream a few years back as I was speaking to a conference of youth leaders from across America. I was sharing what I think is one of the most gripping scenes in Scripture, the account where God meets Moses at the burning bush. As the encounter unfolds, God calls Moses by name and, at Moses's request, reveals His name to humankind for the very first time that we know of. In this amazing divine exchange, God discloses that His name is, in fact, a little offbeat as well, announcing that His name is "I AM WHO I AM." (See Exodus 3:14.)

Simply, it means God exists. God is. God has been, He is in this moment, and He always will be—God!

The point I was trying to get across in my talk is that God is everything we need.

> We have already achieved
> the greatest heights
> because we know I AM.

Yet, while I was speaking, I started having a minirevelation of my own. If God's name is *I AM WHO I AM*, as He confided to Moses, then my name must be *I am not*. After all, by the nature of the name and title *I AM*, the rest of us must be called something else—and that something is *I am not I AM*, or in short, *I am not*.

To say it differently, God's name is *I have always been and always will be God*, and my name is *I have never been and never will be God*. My name is *I am not*.

"Hmm. What's so good about this news?" you may be asking. After all, many of us have spent our lives trying to do more, gain more, become more influential, get ahead, and lead the way. The message of "I am not" *seemingly* comes as an affront to our pursuit of being all we can be and experiencing the very best we can achieve. Yet, the fact that our names are *I am not* does not require us to put ourselves down, but rather to embrace the fact that we have already achieved the greatest heights because we know *I AM.*

Once while I was sharing this message with a friend who was a promising professional athlete, he questioned how this "I am not" way of thinking fit with his goals in the competitive arena. He was struggling with the notion that he was supposed to embrace his smallness, when in fact his sporting role required him to be as big and strong as possible…and hopefully to be tougher, smarter, and faster than the next guy.

You may feel the same way. You have huge dreams and giant goals, and what fuels you on the journey is the belief that *you can* do more, achieve more, be more! In fact, in the cultural space you occupy you may *have* to scratch and claw to stay in the game or to be taken seriously at all.

I went on to share with my young athlete friend that coming to terms with the idea that we are each *I am not* does not mean relinquishing our dreams, setting aside our competitive desires, or settling for less than the best in every area of life. On the contrary, knowing *I AM* inspires

LOUIE GIGLIO

us to excel in every area of life. Further, the power of this "I am not" message is that when we compete, and hopefully win, we can avoid the pitfall of gaining the whole world and yet losing our souls. (See Matthew 16:26.)

As we will soon discover, admitting we are not God—not in control, not running anything, not responsible for everyone's well-being, not the solution for everything and everyone, not at the center of all things—doesn't belittle us; it frees us. For as small as we may be, the truth is we are known and prized by the God of all creation. He knows our name, and we know His. We have been invited into a personal relationship with the infinite *I AM WHO I AM*. What can we ever gain or accomplish that could compete with knowing the Maker and Sustainer of the world *on a first-name basis*? What on our résumés eclipses the fact that we walk with God?

And how does this "I am not but I know I AM" message change our everyday lives?

The pages that follow are an assault on two of the archenemies of the heart, two things I believe all of us wrestle with on some level: stress and meaninglessness. The first, *stress*, gets a stranglehold on us when we move through life feeling like everything (every decision, every answer, every provision, every protection) rests on our shoulders. If we, knowingly or unknowingly, view ourselves as the source of all things for all people, we slowly lose peace of mind and find ourselves staring at the ceiling late into the night trying to figure out how to hold it all together and/or medicating ourselves just to make it through the day.

Why? Because the human frame wasn't created to carry the weight of the world. That's why, in the end, stress kills. It kills laughter. Extinguishes hope. Cracks relationships. Squashes dreams. Robs health. And steals God's praise.

> ## The human frame wasn't created to carry the weight of the world.

The other enemy of the soul, *meaninglessness,* looks quite different from stress yet chokes out life with equal vigor. Meaninglessness woos us into spending our one shot at life on insignificant and trivial things. If we are not vigilant, we drift from God's glorious ambition for our lives, losing sight of anything remotely grand, trading

God-instilled passion for an easier and more often traveled road. And if our hearts aren't awakened by majesty, our lives soon shrink into little bits of nothingness. Our days become filled with drama over the ridiculous; our complaints fly free at the smallest challenge or difficulty; our energy and wealth are consumed by what is fleeting; and our chatter becomes dominated by events, people, and things that won't last much longer than the morning mist.

To both stress and meaninglessness, this book says, "Enough!" Enough of little lives led by little people, crumpling under the weight of stress. And enough of empty ambition masquerading as something grand yet marked by the numbing effects of a vacant heart. And more important, this book bids, "Welcome to the Story of God!" In other words, these pages are an invitation to something more.

I could have opted to write this book as a treatise, a legal document to be debated and defended, or an exhaustive scriptural study. Instead, I chose to tell a story, attempting to unpack this seemingly perplexing little title with narrative accounts and colorful pictures, inviting you into an already-in-motion epic account of a glorious and gracious God.

If you are willing to let go of the idea that life is all about you, you will find yourself breathing in fresh rest and living out more meaning than you've ever dreamed. And if you grasp the hand of the Almighty, and embrace the reality that His hand is holding you, I believe you will sense a tectonic shift of the soul that will reward you with a massive payoff of joy that will surprise and stabilize your heart.

And I promise the title will make more sense in the end!

Waking

Life is the tale of two stories, one tiny and frail, the other eternal and enduring. The tiny one, the story of us, is as brief as the blink of an eye. Yet somehow our infatuation with our own little story—and our determination to make it as big as we possibly can—blinds us to the massive God Story that surrounds us on every side.

It's a little like me being shocked several years ago by the reaction of two of New York City's finest as they motioned me over to their squad cars in the middle of my midmorning run. The first officer's opening line (the exact wording of which, I'm sad to say, cannot be repeated here) led to the inexcusable reply, "What does it *look* like I'm doing?"

I quickly realized I had said the wrong thing (with an ill-advised sarcastic tone), especially to a New York City cop. In a heartbeat, my hands were on the hood of his car and threats of arrest were flying all over the place. I was startled and unnerved, and though by then it was too late, my mouth was firmly shut.

"What does it *look* like I'm doing?"

To make matters worse, all I could produce in the way of identification was a hotel key card—one of those fancy ones that look cool but don't even contain the name and address of the hotel. The whole scene was going downhill fast...

Things had started off innocently enough that morning as I headed out the door of our midtown-Manhattan hotel and began plodding down the sidewalk toward the East River about eight blocks away. But just a few steps into my run, it started to rain. First it was just annoying—an intermittent, spitting kind of rain that was more of an inconvenience than anything else. But then the wind picked up, and a steady, chilling downpour started making things miserable. By now I was well on my way and too far from the hotel to make turning back a sensible option, so I kept running north along the river, pressing on in the driving rain.

I don't know what kind of shape you're in, but when I run, I usually think more about survival than scenery. And when I'm running in a cold downpour, I barely think at all. I certainly don't look around to read a lot of the signs. Thus I wasn't paying much attention when suddenly my path was blocked by a chain-link fence. The battered fence stretched from the riverbank on my right to a concrete lane divider that had been following me on my left. Once again I considered my options. Retracing my steps didn't make sense. What made sense was getting out of the rain. So without thinking I hopped over the lane divider and headed for the shelter of an overpass I now noticed across the way.

As it turns out, the overpass was elevated and continued on ahead of me. Luckily, I could keep running under cover for the foreseeable future. This was good news.

I continued north, not really noticing that the lane to my right had, at some point, become two lanes, and then three. After another mile or so, the traffic in all three lanes was moving slower than I, and a driver in one of the cars was shouting something in my direction. But in the rain and traffic, I couldn't quite make out her words. To be honest, I was trying to ignore her anyway. Then the overpass drifted away to the left, and I was once again exposed to the rain.

Soon I noticed the lower levels of the United Nations buildings on my far left, and just ahead were two police cars parked on a wide concrete median. A single officer sat in each car, their eyes meeting mine as each step I took drew us closer together. Everything seemed to be fine, until my forward progress was interrupted by the piercing *blurp* of one of the officers' sirens and the intense motion of his hand directing me to approach.

It was at that moment that I realized I was running down the middle of the FDR, a six-lane expressway that snakes along the eastside shoreline of Manhattan. No kidding! In all my effort to keep putting one foot in front of the other, somewhat blinded by a steady rain, I hadn't noticed that my haphazard path had now placed me squarely in the middle of a *freeway*! No wonder the officer's first question when I finally splashed to a stop in front of his car was incredulous and unprintable.

I mean, seriously! How can you run down the middle of a New York City freeway and not know it? I think the same way you can live your entire life oblivious to the grand Story of the Creator of the universe, an epic tale that is unfolding all around you. The same way you can spend your days making so much of someone as small and transient as you or me and so little of someone as glorious and eternal as God.

That's why this book is not about you and making your story bigger and better, but about you waking up to the infinitely more massive God Story happening all around you...and about you discovering God's invitation to join Him in it. This book is about looking up to see that there's a Story that was going on long before you arrived on planet earth and that will go on long after you're gone.

God is the central character of this preemptive and

prevailing Story, and He is the central character of this book. Because of who He is, God commands center stage in existence, creation, time, life, history, redemption, and eternity.

It's not as though God has some kind of dictator mentality, a misguided sense of self-worth and importance that demands that everyone salute Him and call Him "Sir." Rather, God is God—the Author and Sustainer of everything. He is Alpha and Omega, the Beginning and the End. All things emanate from Him and terminate in Him. From Him alone, every living thing draws its breath. In Him alone, everything is held together.

He is great and grand beyond our ability to comprehend. And He is center stage in history, in eternity, and in all there is.

It's all about Him, and therefore, it's not about you. In saying that, I am not trying to put you down. Nor am I trying to imply that you don't matter at all. To say it's not about you isn't to suggest that you have no place in the incomparable Story of God. In fact, the opposite is true. Amazingly, you appear on every page of God's Story, existing in His thoughts long before this world was made. But we cannot lose sight of the obvious—the fact that the Story already has a star, and that star is not you or me.

Here's why that matters: if we don't get the two stories straight, everything else in our lives will be out of sync. We'll spend our days trying to hijack the Story of God, turning it into the story of us. Inverting reality, we'll live every day as though life is all about you and me. We'll live like the world is our habitation alone, existence our playground, and God our servant (that is, if we decide we need Him at all). We will throw every ounce of our energy into the fleeting story of us. Calling the shots, our me-centered thinking will dictate every move we make and how we feel.

> The Story already
> has a star, and that
> star is not you or me.

If we're good enough, we'll cobble together a decent little story, one in which the limelight shines on us and on all we have done. Yet in the end—when the last clap is clapped for our tiny tale—our story will fade to black, a pitiful return on our one-shot chance called "life on earth."

About thirty minutes into my ordeal with the New York police officers, the situation lightened a bit as I realized that the worst that was going to happen to me was getting a ticket for jaywalking, something I certainly deserved. As we were waiting for my vital information and my record of wrongdoing to appear on the squad car's computer, the nicer of the two cops asked me within earshot of the other, "So, what do you do for a living, anyway?"

Hmm.

Opting for the short answer, I said, "I'm a pastor."

Two sets of eyebrows rose.

"A pastor!" one of the officers blurted out while they both drew a more inquisitive bead on me. "What kind of pastor are *you*?"

I think he was looking for the name of a denomination, but I simply replied, "I'm a Christian."

"Oh yeah? Well, what are you doing in New York?"

"I'm here to speak to a group of college students tonight in Queens."

Long pause. More staring.

"So, what are you going to tell them?"

For a split second, time stood still. And then I told him, "I'm going to remind them that life is short and our time on earth is really brief. That's why we have to make sure our lives count for the stuff that lasts forever."

And that's what I want to do in these pages. My hope is to lead you to a fresh awareness of the six-lane-wide, freeway-sized God Story that you and I are running down the middle of every day.

It's an awareness that requires a constant choice. We can either choose to cling to starring roles in the little-bitty stories of us or opt to exchange our fleeting moment in the spotlight for a supporting role in the eternally beautiful epic that is the Story of God.

I want to lead you (and me) to that beautiful place of surrender, that place where we give in and give up on the story of us and step up and join in the Story of God's fame.

If such a notion unnerves you from the start, don't think of it as losing. Think of it as trading up.

Abandoning the tiny story of me and embracing the forever Story of Jesus will allow our little lives to be filled with the wonder of God as we live for the unending applause of His name. And joining our small stories to His will give us what we all want most in life, anyway: the assurance that our brief moments on earth will count for something in a Story that never ends.